2003

W9-DBH-327

3 0301 00212237 8

# O Holy Night!

Also by Johann M. Moser

*The Aquinas Prayer Book*
*(with Robert Anderson)*

# O Holy Night!

## Masterworks of Christmas Poetry

Edited by

## Johann M. Moser

### Sophia Institute Press®

Manchester, New Hampshire

LIBRARY
UNIVERSITY OF ST. FRANCIS
JOLIET, ILLINOIS

"The Mother of God" is reprinted with permission of Scribner, a Division of Simon & Schuster, from *The Collected Poems of W. B. Yeats*, Revised Second Edition, edited by Richard J. Finneran. Copyright 1933 by Macmillan Publishing Company; copyright renewed © 1961 by Bertha Georgie Yeats.

"Journey of the Magi" from *Collected Poems 1909-1962* by T. S. Eliot, copyright 1936 by Harcourt, Inc., copyright © 1963, 1964 by T. S. Eliot, is reprinted by permission of the publisher. Permission to reprint this poem from *Collected Poems 1909-1962* by T. S. Eliot is also granted by Faber and Faber Ltd. in the United Kingdom.

"A Christmas Hymn" from *Advice to a Prophet and Other Poems*, copyright © 1961 and renewed 1989 by Richard Wilbur, is reprinted by permission of Harcourt, Inc.

"Sweet is she and gently sworn" is copyright © 1994 Montague Brown, and reprinted by permission of the author.

Permission to publish a new English translation of Boris Pasternak's poem "Christmas Star" is granted by Pantheon Books, a division of Random House, Inc.

Copyright © 1995 Johann Moser

Printed in the United States of America

All rights reserved

Jacket design by Lorraine Bilodeau

On the jacket is George Spencer Watson's *The Three Wise Kings* (photo courtesy of Rochdale Art Gallery, Lancashire, United Kingdom / Bridgeman Art Library).

No part of this book may be reproduced, stored in a retrieval system, or transmitted in any form, or by any means, electronic, mechanical, photocopying, or otherwise, without the prior written permission of the publisher, except by a reviewer, who may quote brief passages in a review.

Sophia Institute Press®

Box 5284, Manchester, NH 03108

1-800-888-9344

www.sophiainstitute.com

Library of Congress Cataloging-in-Publication Data

O Holy Night! : Masterworks of Christmas Poetry / selected and edited by Johann M. Moser.
    p.  cm.
  Includes bibliographical references.
  ISBN 0-918477-24-7
  1. Christmas—Poetry.    I. Moser, Johann, 1940-
PN6110.C5015    1995
808.81'933—dc20
                                             94-34707    CIP

01 02 03 04 10 9 8 7 6 5 4

808.81933
0110

# CONTENTS

*Psalm 110*

---

PART I

## THE PRINCE OF PEACE

*Wisdom 18:14-15*

*Isaiah 9:6*

*John 1:1-5*

*Luke 1:68-79*

PART II

# A WOMAN CLOTHED WITH THE SUN

*Isaiah 7:14*

*Psalm 45:13-15*

*Luke 1:31-33*

*Luke 1:46-55*

---

PART III

# O GREAT MYSTERY!

*Psalm 2:7-8*

*Isaiah 45:8*

*Luke 2:6-14*

*Psalm 148*

---

PART IV

# BRIGHT STAR OF JACOB

*Numbers 24:17*

*Psalm 72:6-8, 10, 16-17*

*Matthew 2: 9-11*

*Luke 2:29-32*

*Colossians 1:15-17*

# Preface

Even a very superficial perusal of the European lyrical verse tradition reveals a substantial number of fine poems, often by authors of note, which are devoted to the celebration of Christ's Nativity. Indeed, so impressive is this achievement that it engenders the irresistible urge to bring many of these poems together into a single collection. Two purposes are served by such a collection: first, it can give to a serious literary public a sense of the richness, variety, and artistic excellence that characterizes the tradition of Nativity poetry; secondly, it furnishes readers with a cultivated resource for meditating on the mystery of the Holy Night.

In this collection, I have attempted to select out of the vast store of Nativity verse those works which exhibit the highest degree of artistic merit and interest. On occasion, fidelity to this consideration has induced me to include excerpts from longer works, rather than to present the entire works themselves. Also included are various passages from homiletic prose literature which are possessed of an unusually high poetic quality. Unless otherwise noted, all translations are my own. In translating many of the poems, I have made an effort to convey those features of a work which, I felt, had the richest possibilities for producing a successful poem in English.

The anthology is divided into four sections (corresponding to Advent, the Blessed Virgin, Bethlehem, the Magi) and each of these sections is framed with passages from the Old and New Testaments and from the tradition of Christian homiletic and liturgical literature. Hence, the collection as a whole resembles the ancient service of Lessons and Carols as it is still practiced in some churches today and which has its origin in the rites of the canonical hours as performed in medieval monasteries and cathedrals.

At the end of the collection are several appendices for those who would be inclined to explore the chronological relationships of the works with one another, as well as with works which, for various reasons, I could not include. The evolution of the Nativity lyric in itself would be a most fruitful topic for scholarly investigation. Though the purpose of the present collection is to provide neither a history of the Nativity poem, nor a thorough scholarly compendium of all materials potentially relevant to such a history, I do hope that it might inspire scholars to prepare such compendia and to furnish them with the erudite commentary that they would certainly merit.

I would like to extend my gratitude to colleagues at St. Anselm College who have been of invaluable assistance in bringing this anthology to fruition: to Paul Vyrros of the Department of Modern Languages for help in finding and translating Spanish poems; to John Windhausen of the History Department for guidance in working with Pasternak's Russian; to Elona Lucas, Gary Bouchard, and Father Thomas Kass of the English Department for their comments and suggestions; to Maureen McCabe; to Brother Andrew Thornton, O.S.B.; to John Barger and Kelley Spoerl of Sophia Institute Press; and to Ken Walker for his patience in introducing me to the world of word processing technology. I would also like to thank my daughter Antonia for aid in translating the Dutch of Constantijn Huygens.

Johann M. Moser<br>
St. Anselm College

# O Holy Night!

AT THE MOMENT
OF THY PRINCELY DOMINION
THY PEOPLE SHALL FLOCK
TO THEE
ADORNED IN THE SPLENDOR
OF THY HOLY ONES;

IN THE DEW OF THY YOUTH
I HAVE BEGOTTEN THEE,
EVEN AS THE DAY-STAR
IN THE WOMB OF MORNING.

THE LORD HAS PROMISED;
HE SHALL NOT FORSWEAR:
THOU ART
A PRIEST FOREVER.


Psalm 110

PART I

# THE PRINCE OF PEACE

WHILE ALL THINGS
WERE IN DEEPEST SILENCE
AND NIGHT WAS IN THE MIDST
OF HER SWIFT COURSE,
YOUR ALMIGHTY WORD, O LORD,
LEAPT DOWN
FROM YOUR ROYAL THRONE,
ALLELUIA.

Wisdom 18:14-15

*For unto us a Child is born,*
*Unto us a Son is given.*
*And Dominion rests*
*Upon His Shoulders,*
*And they shall call Him:*
*Wondrous Counsellor,*
*God-Victorious,*
*Father Everlasting,*
*The Prince of Peace.*

Isaiah 9:6

*In the beginning was the Word,*
*And the Word was with God,*
*And the Word was God.*
*He was in the beginning with God.*
*All things were made through Him.*
*And without Him was made*
*Nothing that has been made.*
*In Him there was life,*
*And that life was the light of men.*
*And that light shines in the darkness,*
*And the darkness could not vanquish it.*

John 1:1-5

# "If some king of the earth"

If some king of the earth
Have so large an extent of dominion,
    in north and south,
As that he hath winter and summer
    together in his dominions;

So large an extent east and west,
As that he hath day and night,
    together in his dominions;
Much more hath God
    mercy and judgment together.

He brought light out of darkness,
    not out of a lesser light;
He can bring thy summer out of winter,
    though thou have no spring.

Though in the ways of fortune,
    or understanding, or conscience,
Thou have been benighted till now,
    wintered and frozen,
    clouded and eclipsed,
    damped and benumbed,
    smothered and stupefied till now,

Now God comes to thee,
    not as in the dawning of the day,
    not as in the bud of the spring,
But as the sun at noon to illustrate all shadows,
As the sheaves in harvest to fill all penuries.

All occasions invite his mercies,
And all times are his seasons.

*John Donne* (1572-1631)
*Sermon for Christmas Day 1624*

*from*
# The Fourth Eclogue

Sicilian Muse, begin a loftier strain!
Tho' lowly shrubs and trees that shade the plain,
Delight not all; Sicilian Muse, prepare
To make the vocal woods deserve a consul's care.
The last great age, foretold by sacred rhymes
Renews its finished course; Saturnian times
Roll round again, and mighty years, begun
From their first orb, in radiant circles run.
The base degenerate iron offspring ends;
A golden progeny from heav'n descends:
O chaste Lucina, speed the mother's pains;
And haste the glorious Birth; thy own Apollo reigns!
The lovely boy, with his auspicious face,
Shall Pollio's consulship and triumph grace;
Majestic months set out with him to their appointed race.
The father banished virtue shall restore,
And crimes shall threat the guilty world no more.
The son shall lead the life of gods and be
By gods and heros seen and gods and heros see.
The jarring nations he in peace shall bind,
And with paternal virtues rule mankind.
Unbidden earth shall wreathing ivy bring,
And fragrant herbs (the promises of spring)
As her first offerings to her infant king.
The goats with strutting dugs shall homeward speed,
And lowing herds secure from lions feed.

His cradle shall with rising flowers be crowned;
The serpent's brood shall die: the sacred ground
Shall weeds and pois'nous plants refuse to bear,
Each common bush shall Syrian roses wear.
But when heroic verse his youth shall raise
And form it to hereditary praise;
Unlabored harvests shall the fields adorn,
And clustered grapes shall blush on every thorn.
The knotted oaks shall showers of honey weep,
And through the matted grass the liquid gold shall creep.

*Virgil*
*(70-19 B.C.)*

*Note: This is a translation by John Dryden (1631-1700), who*
*wrote "Many of the verses are translated from one of the Sybils,*
*who prophesied of our Saviour's birth."*

## "Gideon's threshing floor"

*Gedeonis area*
*celitus perfusa rore*
*flamma rubis ignea*
*radiat absque calore.*
*Nucleum ex nuclea*
*testa prodit lutea,*
*lux aurea!*
*Granum exit palea,*
*oleatris olea,*
*liquitur petra liquore.*

Gideon's threshing floor
Is drenched with heavenly dew.
In the burning bramble-bush
The flame glows without heat.
An earthen vessel
Brings forth a seed from a seed,
O golden splendor!
The grain springs from the chaff,
The olive from the olive trees,
And the rock overflows with water.

*Advent Processional Hymn*
*(1200s)*

# The Birth Night of the Lord

O Night! Great Night! brighter than the day!
O Night! Yes, Light! Light which outshines the sun!
O Night! Which cosmic orbits never did convey!
O Night! In which the greatest miracle is won!

O Night! Whom Patriarchs' speech did ever grace!
O Night! When cliff and mountain shall resound!
O Night! Embracing Him whom nothing can embrace!
O Night! To whose child all kneel upon the ground!

O Night! The Heavens tremble at its course!
O Night! Whose moon, the moon and sun did trim!
O Night! Which glows where moon and sun do hymn!
O Night! Which outshines the Cherubic force!
O Night! I shall watch your constellations grand,
Until my soul arises to join that starry band!

*Quirinus Kuhlmann*
*(1651-1689)*

# The Advent Antiphons

O SAPIENTIA,
QUAE EX ORE ALTISSIMI PRODIISTI,

O Wisdom,
that came forth from the mouth of the Most High,
extending from one end of the universe to the other,
mightily and deftly ordaining all things:
*come,*
teach us the way of sagacity.

O ADONAI,
ET DUX DOMUS ISRAEL,

O Adonai,
and Prince of the House of Israel,
who appeared to Moses in the flames of a burning bush
and bestowed on him the Law upon Sinai:
*come,*
ransom us with outstretched arm.

O RADIX JESSE,
QUI STAS IN SIGNUM POPULORUM,

O Stem of Jesse,
who stands forth as a sign unto all peoples,
before whom the kings of the earth shall be silent,
whom the nations shall invoke in prayer:
*come,*
deliver us, tarry no longer.

O CLAVIS DAVID,
ET SCEPTRUM DOMUS ISRAEL,

O Key of David,
and Scepter of the House of Israel,
who opens, and no man closes;
who shuts and no man opens:
*come,*
bring forth from the house of captivity the vanquished,
who sit in darkness and the shadow of death.

O ORIENS,
SPLENDOR LUCIS AETERNAE,
ET SOL JUSTITIAE,

O Day-Spring,
Splendor of Eternal Light,
and Sun of Justice:
*come,*
enlighten those who sit in darkness
and in the shadow of death.

O EMMANUEL,
REX ET LEGIFER NOSTER,

O Emmanuel,
King and our Lawgiver,
the Desire of all nations and their Savior:
*come,*
save us, Lord, our God.

*Roman Antiphonary*
*(early 600s)*

## Earendael

*Eala Earendael,*
     *engla beorhtast*
*ofer middangeard*
     *monnum sended*
*ond sothfaesta*
     *sunnan leoma,*
*torht ofer tunglas,*
     *thu tida gehwane*
*of selfum the*
     *symle inlihtes.*

Hail Dawn-Herald!
     Brightest of Angels!
Over the middle-earth
     sent unto men
Most righteous gleam
     of the bounteous sun,
Radiant beyond the stars above.
     All times and seasons
Thou dost illumine
     out of thy innermost depths.
If Thou, O God from God,
     begotten of old before the ages,
Son of the Father,
     have lived forever
Amid the glories of heaven,
     now thine own handiwork

Bids Thee in boldness
  to bestow upon us
This brightest of suns,
  in the time of our need,
To enlighten us who long since,
  have dwelt in perpetual night,
Enfolded in darkness and mist,
  and who have endured
The shades of death and sin.

*Cynewulf* *(c. 800)*
*from "The Advent Lyrics"*

## "Born of the Father's heart"

Born of the Father's heart
    Before the creation of the world,
Alpha and Omega named,
    Beginning and End of all that is,
He commanded and they were made,
    He spoke and they were fashioned:
Earth, heavens, the ocean depths,
    The three-fold spheres of the universe
And all that dwell in them
    Under the lofty sun and moon.
He took upon Himself the shape of man
    Limbs subject to the thrall of death,
That the seed of Adam might not perish
    Whom the dreadful law had plunged
Into the depths of Tartarus.
    O blessed that sacred birth!—
When the child-bearing Virgin
    Having conceived of the Holy Spirit,
Brought forth our salvation,
    And the Child, Redeemer of the world,
Revealed His sacred countenance.
    Sing, O vast heights of the heavens!
Sing, Angels, all powers that be!
    Sing, prophets, as you once foretold!
Let all things join in praising Him!
    Old men and young, choirs of children,

Mothers, virgins, infant girls,
     Praise Him with harmonious voices;
Let the turbulent rivers praise
     And the thunderous shores of the sea,
The storms and rain, the summer heat,
     Frost, snow, the forest breeze,
Day and night, let all unite,
     All celebrate His glory for evermore.

*Prudentius*
*(348-413)*

# A Child of the Snows

There is heard a hymn when the panes are dim
    And never before or again,
When the nights are strong with a darkness long,
    And the dark is alive with rain.

Never we know but in sleet and in snow,
    The place where the great fires are,
That the midst of the earth is a raging mirth
    And the heart of the earth a star.

And at night we win to the ancient inn
    Where the child in the frost is furled,
We follow the feet where all souls meet
    At the inn at the end of the world.

The gods lie dead where the leaves lie red,
    For the flame of the sun is flown,
The gods lie cold where the leaves lie gold,
    And a Child comes forth alone.

*G. K. Chesterton*
*(1874-1936)*

# On the Birth of Jesus

Night more than starry night! Night lighter than the day!
Night brighter than the sun wherein the light is born;
Which God, the light, who lives in light, chose as his own!
O Night which all days and nights now comfort may!

O joyous Night wherein our deepest woe and sorrow
And darkness deep and worldly plottings dire
And dread and fear of Hell and horror shall expire!
Heaven bursts, but no thunder strikes tomorrow.

The Maker of days and nights this night has come,
Time's realm and human body to assume,
Bequeathing both flesh and time to eternal bloom.
The mournful night, the black night of our sins,
Darkness of the sepulchre shall vanish in this night.
Night lighter than the day! Night more than starry night!

*Andreas Gryphius*
*(1616-1664)*

# "We do not only proclaim one coming of Christ"

We do not only proclaim one coming of Christ,
    but a second as well,
        and that much more glorious than the first.

For the first bore with it the sign of suffering;
    the second will confer the diadem of the divine kingdom.

For He was born from God before all ages;
    and He was born from a Virgin in the consummation of time.

He came hidden like rain upon a fleece;
    He will come in the lateness of days, manifest to all creation.

At His first coming He was wrapped
    in swaddling clothes in a manger;
At His second coming He shall be garbed
    in the vestments of heavenly light.

In His first coming He endured the cross
    and was spurned in shame;
In His second coming He will be glorified,
    in the company of hosts of angels.

Therefore we repose not only in the first coming,
    but we eagerly await the second.

At the first coming we said,
    *"Blessed is He who comes in the name of the Lord."*
At the second we shall say it again,
    when with the angels we shall rush to greet Him,
And we will cry out in adoration,
    *"Blessed is He who comes in the name of the Lord."*

*St. Cyril of Jerusalem*
*(315-386)*

*Blessed be the Lord, the God of Israel,*
*because He has visited and redeemed His people.*

*He has raised up for us a Horn of Salvation*
*in the House of David His servant,*
*as He promised through the lips of His holy ones,*
*the prophets from of old.*

*He has saved us from our enemies*
*and from the hands of those who hate us.*
*He has shown mercy to our fathers*
*and has remembered His holy covenant,*
*the promise that He made to Abraham our father,*
*that, delivered from fear and the hands of our foes,*
*we should serve Him in holiness and justice*
*all the days of our lives in His presence.*

*And you, holy child, shall be called*
*a prophet of the Most High,*
*and you shall go before the Lord*
*to prepare His ways and make known to His people*
*their salvation in the forgiveness of sins;*

*Through the kindness of our God,*
*he shall visit us like the dawn from on high.*
*He shall enlighten those who sit in darkness*
*and in the valley of death,*
*and He shall guide us into the ways of peace.*

Luke 1:68-79
*The Song of Zachariah*

# PART II

# A WOMAN CLOTHED WITH THE SUN

BEHOLD A VIRGIN SHALL CONCEIVE
AND BEAR A SON
AND HIS NAME SHALL BE CALLED
EMMANUEL.

Isaiah 7:14

LIBRARY
UNIVERSITY OF ST. FRANCIS
JOLIET, ILLINOIS

*All glorious*
*is the king's daughter in her chamber;*
*her raiment is woven with spun gold.*

*Clad in embroidered apparel,*
*she is led before the king;*
*behind her, the virgins of her retinue*
*are brought unto you.*

*With gladness and joy,*
*they enter the palace of the king.*

Psalm 45:13-15

*Behold,*
*you shall conceive*
*in your womb*
*and shall bring forth a son,*
*and you shall call His name Jesus.*

*He shall be great*
*and shall be called*
*the Son of the Most High;*
*and the Lord God shall give Him*
*the throne of David his father.*

*And He shall reign*
*over the House of Jacob in eternity;*
*and his Kingdom shall be without end.*

Luke 1:31-33

## "A spotless Rose is blooming"

*Es ist ein Ros entsprungen*
*aus einer Wurzel zart,*
*als uns die Alten sungen,*
*aus Jesse kam die Art,*
*und hat ein Blümlein bracht,*
*mitten in kaltem Winter,*
*wohl zu der halben Nacht.*

*Das Röslein, das ich meine,*
*darvon Esaias sagt,*
*hat uns gebracht alleine*
*Marie die reine Magd;*
*aus Gottes ewgem Rat*
*hat sie ein Kind geboren*
*wohl zu der halben Nacht.*

A spotless Rose is blooming
Sprung from a tender root.
Of ancient seers foreshowing
Of Jesse's promised fruit.
Its fairest bud unfolds to light
Amid the cold, cold winter
And in the dark midnight.

The Rose which I am singing
Whereof Isaiah said,
Is from its sweet root springing
In Mary, purest maid.
For, through God's great love and might,
The blessed Babe she bare us
In a cold, cold winter's night.

*Anonymous*
*(1500s)*

# "A *Virgin* shall conceive, a *Virgin* bear a Son!"

A *Virgin* shall conceive, a *Virgin* bear a Son!
From *Jesse's* root behold a Branch arise,
Whose sacred Flow'r with Fragrance fills the Skies.
Th' Aethereal Spirit o'er its Leaves shall move,
And on its Top descends the Mystic Dove.
Ye Heav'ns! from high the dewy Nectar pour,
And in soft Silence shed the kindly Show'r!
The Sick and Weak the healing Plant shall aid;
From Storms a Shelter, and from Heat a Shade.
All Crimes shall cease, and ancient Fraud shall fail;
Returning Justice lift aloft her Scale;
Peace o'er the World her Olive-Wand extend,
And white-rob'd Innocence from Heav'n descend.
Swift fly the Years, and rise th'expected Morn!
Oh spring to Light, Auspicious Babe, be born!

*Alexander Pope (1688-1744)*
*from "Messiah: A Sacred Eclogue"*

# "Faithful choir, rejoicing sing"

Faithful choir, rejoicing sing
    *Alleluia!*
A Virgin bore the King of Kings,
O most wondrous thing!
    *Alleluia!*

From the Virgin's womb,
    *Alleluia!*
The Angel of Great Counsel comes,
From a star, the Sun at noon—
    *Alleluia!*

That Sun which shall never set,
    *Alleluia!*
That Star shall grow brighter yet,
One the other's coronet,
    *Alleluia!*

The towering Cedar of Lebanon,
    *Alleluia!*
The hyssop of the vale has drawn,
To this resplendent dawn,
    *Alleluia!*

*St. Bernard of Clairvaux*
*(1090-1153)*

# "*Salut,* woman in splendor upon her knees"

*Salut,* woman in splendor upon her knees,
    first-born before all creatures!
The infinite depths were not as yet,
    and yet you were conceived!
It was you who made an undiminishing brilliance
    to shine in the Heavens!
When He made a cross over the abyss,
    the All-Mighty One had your image before Him,
As I have it before me in my heart,
    O incomparable *Fleur-de-lys,* Virgin pure!
You have borne your Creator, you have
    engendered Him in the girth of your being.
Mary, our sister, in your faith you have encompassed
    the Man from every side.
The unclad infant snuggles close on your breast,
    O Theotokos, God-Bearer!
Like the Son on the bosom of the Ancient of Days,
    to Whom is the Kingdom, the Eternal Amen!
O lucid Paradise of God, draw us by the aromas
    of your healing balms!
As He was Himself Who out of all Eternity longed
    for the sweetness of your milk,
And who said, "Receive Me, My sister,
    My dove, My friend, My immaculate one!"
Yield forth at last the Man to His God,
    O royal portal now unsealed!
O heart of the torrents of darkness in whom,
    with ineffable consent,
The silver hue of the dove commingles
    with the lustre of gold.

*Paul Claudel*
*(1868-1955)*

# "I sing of a maiden"

I sing of a maiden
That is makeles;
King of alle kinges
To here son she ches.

He cam also stille
There his moder was
As dew in Aprille
That falleth on the grass.

He cam also stille
To his moderes bowr,
As dew in Aprille
That falleth on the flowr.

He cam also stille
There his moder lay,
As dew in Aprille
That falleth on the spray.

Moder and maiden
Was never non but she;
Well may swich a lady
Godes moder be.

*Anonymous*
*(early 1400s)*

# "Of her flesh He took flesh"

Of her flesh he took flesh:
He does take fresh and fresh,
Though much the mystery how,
Not flesh but spirit now
And makes, O marvelous!
New Nazareths in us,
Where she shall yet conceive
Him, morning, noon, and eve;
New Bethlems, and he born
There, evening, noon, and morn—
Bethlem or Nazareth,
Men here may draw like breath
More Christ and baffle death;
Who, born so, comes to be
New self and nobler me
In each one and each one
More makes, when all is done,
Both God's and Mary's Son.

*Gerard Manley Hopkins, S.J.* (1844-1889)

*from "The Blessed Virgin compared
to the Air we Breathe"*

# "Underneath this crag is born"

*Underneath this crag is born*
*A Rose that scorches not the sky.*

Underneath a rough-hewn arch
A divine Rose-Branch is growing;
Beside it resides a queen,
Of angelic eyes and gracious mien.

This queen of beauteous countenance
Has nurtured here a Rose
Of such loveliness and splendor
That none has seen its like before.

O Rose so white and many-hued,
O Rose so blessed and sanctified,
O Rose through Whom is now atoned
Our primal father's ancient sin.

Like the Holy Virgin Mary
Is the Rose-Branch I have sung;
The Rose which she brought forth
Is her Father, Spouse, and Son.

It is the Rose of our Salvation,
Granted to redeem us here,
To heal the old world's painful doom,
Our primal mother's ancient wound.

*Underneath this crag is born*
*A Rose that scorches not the sky.*

*Esteban de Zafra*
*(c. 1595)*

## O Gloriosa Domina

Hail most high, most humble one!
Above the world; below thy Son,
Whose blush the moon beauteously mars
And stains the timorous light of stars.
He that made all things, had not done,
Till He had made Himself thy son.
The whole world's Host would be thy guest
And board Himself at thy rich breast.
O boundless hospitality!
The Feast of all things feeds on thee.

Let hearts and lips speak loud and say
Hail door of life and source of day!
The door was shut, the fountain sealed;
Yet light was seen and life revealed.
The door was shut, yet let in day,
The fountain sealed, yet life found way.
Glory to Thee, great virgin's Son,
In bosom of thy Father's bliss.
The same to Thee, sweet Spirit be done.
As ever shall be, was, and is.

*Richard Crashaw*
*(1612-1649)*

## Ave Maria Gratia Plena

Was this His coming! I had hoped to see
A scene of wondrous glory, as was told
Of some great God who in a rain of gold
Broke open bars and fell on Danaë:
Or a dread vision as when Semele,
Sickening for love and unappeased desire,
Prayed to see God's clear body, and the fire
Caught her brown limbs and slew her utterly.
With such glad dreams I sought this holy place,
And now with wondering eyes and heart I stand
Before this supreme mystery of Love:
Some kneeling girl with passionless pale face,
An angel with a lily in his hand,
And over both the white wings of a dove.

*Oscar Wilde*
*(1854-1900)*

## Rosa Mystica

There is no rose of such virtu
As is the rose that bear Jesu:
  *Alleluia.*

For in this rose contained was
Heaven and earth in little space:
  *Res miranda.*

By that rose we may well see
There be one God in Persons Three:
  *Pares forma.*

The angels sang, the shepherds too:
*Gloria in excelsis Deo:*
  *Gaudeamus.*

Leave we all this world's mirth
And follow we this joyful birth:
  *Transeamus.*

  *Anonymous*
  *(1400s)*

# "There comes a ship so laden"

There comes a ship so laden
Where highest decks engird:
It brings the Father's Son,
The true, Eternal Word.

Over the quiet ocean waves
The vessel sails serene.
It brings to us a precious gift,
A right and noble Queen.

Maria, O you noble Rose,
O branch of every pleasantry,
You lovely lily-flower,
From sin make us now free.

The little ship sails silently
And brings such treasure vast;
The sails are made of love,
The Holy Spirit is the mast.

*Johannes Tauler, O.P.*
*(1300-1371)*

# Annunciation

*Salvation to all that will is nigh,*
That All, which always is all everywhere,
Which cannot sin, and yet all sins must bear,
Which cannot die, yet cannot choose but die,
Lo, faithful Virgin, yields himself to lie
In prison, in thy womb; and though he there
Can take no sin, nor thou give, yet he will wear
Taken from thence, flesh, which death's force may try.
Ere by the spheres time was created, thou
Wast in his mind, who is thy Son, and Brother,
Whom thou conceiv'st, conceiv'd; yea thou art now
Thy Maker's maker, and thy Father's mother,
Thou hast light in dark; and shutst in little room,
*Immensity cloistered in thy dear womb.*

*John Donne* (1572-1631)
*from La Corona*

## "Heaven rejoice! Earth clap your hands!"

Heaven rejoice! Earth clap your hands!
Let none refrain from praise!
Through a maid mankind returns
To its primordial origins!

You are the Window, Gate, and Fleece,
The Palace, Household, Temple, Earth,
The Lily of Virginity,
And Rose of all the martyrs.

You are the Queen of Angels,
The Hope for God from age to age,
The Royal Couch for a new-born King,
The Throne of Divinity.

O Star glimmering in the East,
Pursuing shades into the West
O Dawn before the Sun proceeding,
And Day unknown to night!

*Peter the Venerable*
*(d. 1155)*

# "Yo no tengo soledad"

## 1

This night is without solace
From the mountains to the sea.
But I, who am rocking you,
I am not alone!
*Yo no tengo soledad!*

The sky is without solace,
Since the moon falls into the sea.
But I, who cradle you in my arms,
I am not alone!
*Yo no tengo soledad!*

The world is without solace,
All flesh goes sadly.
But I, who hold you close,
I am not alone!
*Yo no tengo soledad!*

## 2

The sea rocks divinely
Its many thousands of waves.
Listening to the loving seas,
I rock my child.
*Mezo a mi niño.*

The wind wandering in the night
Rocks the grain-fields.
Listening to the loving winds,
I rock my child.
*Mezo a mi niño.*

God the Father rocks silently
His many thousands of worlds.
Feeling His hand in the shadows,
I rock my child.
  *Mezo a mi niño.*


                    3


I found this child
When I was going into the fields.
I found him sleeping
Among some ears of corn . . .
  *En unas espigas.*

Or perhaps I found him
While crossing the vineyards;
While groping through the tendrils,
I glanced his cheek . . .
  *Tope su mejilla.*

And for this reason I'm afraid
Should I fall asleep,
That he might melt away
Like frost among the vineyards . . .
  *La helada en las viñas.*


    *Gabriela Mistral*
    *(1889-1957)*

# The Mother of God

The threefold terror of love; a fallen flare
Through the hollow of an ear;
Wings beating about the room;
The terror of all terrors that I bore
The Heavens in my womb.

Had I not found content among the shows
Every common woman knows,
Chimney corner, garden walk,
Or rocky cistern where we tread the clothes
And gather all the talk?

What is this flesh I purchased with my pains,
This fallen star my milk sustains,
This love which makes my heart's blood stop
Or strikes a sudden chill into my bones
And bids my hair stand up?

*William Butler Yeats*
*(1865-1939)*

# "Virgin mother, daughter of thy son"

*Vergine Madre, figlia del tuo figlio,*
*umile e alta più che creatura,*
*termine fisso d'etterno consiglio,*

*tu se' colei che l'umana natura*
*nobilitasti sì, che 'l suo fattore*
*non disdegnò de farsi sua fattura.*

*Nel ventre tuo si raccese l'amore*
*per lo cui caldo nell'etterna pace*
*così è germinato questo fiore.*

*Qui se' a noi meridiana face*
*de caritate, e giuso, intra i mortali,*
*se' di speranza fontana vivace.*

Virgin mother, daughter of thy son,
      humblest of all things and yet most high,
      Eternal Counsel's peerless paragon,

thou alone could truly dignify
      human nature, so that by its making
      our Maker to be made would not deny.

In thy womb that love was just awaking
      in whose warmth this heavenly Rose
      eternal peace shall ever be partaking.

Here the zenith's torch thou dost disclose
      of charity; in thou, among the living yet,
      Springs of hope shall evermore repose.

*Dante Alighieri* (1265-1321)
*From the Paradiso, XXXIII, 1-12*

*from*
## Invocacio ad Mariam

Thou Maid and Mother, daughter of thy Son,
Thou well of mercy, our sinful souls' cure,
In whom God for goodness chose to dwell;
Thou humble one, yet high over each creature,
Thou makest noble henceforth our nature
That no disdain the Maker had of kind
His Son in blood and flesh to clothe and wind.

Within the blissful cloister of thy sides
Took man's shape the eternal love and peace,
That of the threefold world both Lord and guide is,
Whom earth and sea and heaven, without cease,
Still praise; and thou, Virgin from all flaw secure,
Bore of thy body—and remained a maiden pure—
The Creator of every creature.

Assembled is in thee magnificence
With mercy, goodness, and with such pity
That thou, that art the sun of excellence
Not only helpeth them that pray to thee,
But often times, of thy benignity,
Full freely, ere men to thine own help appeal,
Thou goest before, and dost their souls heal.

*Geoffrey Chaucer*
*(1343-1400)*

*My soul magnifies the Lord,*
*and my spirit has found joy in God*
*who is my salvation,*
*because He has looked with favor*
*upon the lowliness of His servant.*

*Behold, from this day forward*
*all ages shall call me blessed, because He who is mighty*
*has done great things for me, and His name is holy;*
*from age to age His mercy is on those who fear Him.*

*He wielded power with His arm*
*and has dispersed the proud in the folly of their hearts.*
*He has brought down the mighty from their thrones*
*and has exalted the humble.*

*He has filled the hungry with good things,*
*and has sent the rich away empty.*

*He has upheld his servant Israel,*
*mindful of His mercies from of old,*
*even as He promised to our fathers,*
*to Abraham and to his posterity forever.*

Luke 1:46-55
*The Magnificat*

PART III

# O GREAT MYSTERY!

YOU ARE MY SON;
THIS DAY I HAVE BEGOTTEN YOU.

ASK AND I SHALL GIVE YOU
THE NATIONS AS YOUR INHERITANCE
AND THE ENDS OF THE EARTH
AS YOUR POSSESSION.

Psalm 2:7-8

*Drop down dew, O heavens.*
*Let justice shower from the skies.*
*Let the earth open, and bring forth a Savior;*
*Let righteousness bud together with Him:*
*For I, the Lord, have created Him.*

Isaiah 45:8

*And it happened while they were there,*
*that the time for her delivery came to pass.*
*She brought forth her firstborn son, and wrapped him*
*in swaddling clothes, and laid him in a manger,*
*because there was no room for them in the inn.*

*In that same country there were shepherds awake*
*in the fields and keeping watch over their flock by night.*
*Behold, an angel of the Lord stood next to them*
*and the glory of God encompassed them,*
*and they were afraid.*

*And the angel said to them,*
*"Do not be afraid, for I bring you tidings of great joy*
*for all peoples; for today in the city of David*
*a Savior has been born for you, who is Christ the Lord.*
*And this shall be a sign for you: you will find a child*
*wrapped in swaddling clothes and lying in a manger."*

*Suddenly with the angel was a multitude*
*of the heavenly host praising God and saying,*
*"Glory to God in the highest,*
*and peace on earth to men of good will."*

Luke 2:6-14

# O Great Mystery!

*O magnum mysterium*
*et admirabile sacramentum:*
*ut animalia viderent Dominum natum*
*jacentum in praesipio.*
*Beata virgo cuius viscera meruerunt*
*portare Dominum Christum.*

O great mystery!
O sacrament most wonderful!—
That animals should see the Lord new born
Lying in a manger.
Blessed is the Virgin whose womb was worthy
To bring forth Christ the Lord!

*Matins of Christmas*
*(Responsory V)*

# "The heavens were made honey-sweet"

Indeed, under the reign of Caesar Augustus,
the quiet silence of universal peace brought such serenity
to an age previously so distressed that through his decree
a census of the whole world could be taken.

The solicitude of divine providence brought it about
that Joseph, the Virgin's husband, took to the city
of Bethlehem the maiden of royal lineage who was with child.

And when nine months had passed since his conception,
*the King of Peace like a spouse from his bridal chamber,*
came forth from the virginal womb.

Although he was great and rich,
he made himself small and poor for us.
He chose to be born not in a house but in a lowly dwelling,
to be wrapped in swaddling clothes, to be fed by virginal milk,
and to be lain in a manger between an ox and an ass.

Then "there shone for us a day of a new redemption,
a restoration of past ages and the happiness of eternity.
Then through the whole world the heavens were made honey-sweet."

*St. Bonaventure (1221-1274)*
*Lignum Vitae I, 4*

# A Hymn on the Nativity of my Saviour

I sing the birth, was born tonight,
The author both of life, and light;
     The angels so did sound it,
And like the ravished shepherds said,
Who saw the light, and were afraid,
     Yet searched, and true they found it.

The Son of God, the Eternal King,
That did us all salvation bring,
     And freed the soul from danger;
He whom the whole world could not take,
The Word, which heaven and earth did make;
     Was laid now in a manger.

The Father's wisdom willed it so,
The Son's obedience knew no no,
     Both wills were in one stature;
And as that Wisdom had decreed,
The Word was now made Flesh indeed,
     And took on Him our nature.

What comfort by Him do we win,
Who made Himself the price of sin,
     To make us heirs of glory?
To see this babe, all innocence;
A martyr born in our defense;
     Can man forget this story?

*Ben Jonson*
*(1573-1637)*

# On the Nativity of Our Lord

O mystery, from whom fertile wonders rise!
O mortals, open here your hearts and eyes;
O purest Seraphim, angelic squadrons bright,
Swoop down to earth in your ardent flight.

He whose praises night and day you hail,
Has left meanwhile his far celestial home;
His robe of light is hid beneath an infant's veil,
A rooftop vile exchanged for his palatial dome.

The Ancient of Days in childhood is concealed,
The unseen seen, and God in birth revealed,
The immortal is now mortal, Infinity is bound.
At last I see you in a lowly stable found;
And ravished I cry out, "Eternal One, born anew!
In your deep humility, how I worship you!"

*Laurent Drelincourt*
*(1626-1681)*

# "No, we must not sleep"

*No la debemos dormir*
*la noche santa,*
*no la debemos dormir.*

*La Virgen a solas piensa*
*qué hará*
*cuando al Rey de luz immensa*
*parirá,*
*si de su divina esencia*
*temblará,*
*o que le podrá decir.*

*No la debemos dormir*
*la noche santa,*
*no la debemos dormir.*

No, we must not sleep
This holy night;
We must not sleep.

The Virgin, all alone, is thinking:
What will she do
When she gives birth
To the King of Immeasurable Light;
If, before His Divine Essence,
She will tremble.
O what will she say to Him?

No, we must not sleep
This holy night;
We must not sleep.

*Fray Ambrosio Montesino*
*(c. 1500)*

# The Burning Babe

As I in hoary Winter's night
    Stood shivering in the snow
Surprised I was with sudden heat
    Which made my heart to glow.

And lifting up a fearful eye
    To view what fire was near,
A pretty Babe all burning bright
    Did in the air appear;

Who, scorched with excessive heat,
    Such floods of tears did shed,
As though his floods should quench his flames,
    Which with his tears were fed:

Alas (quoth he) but newly born,
    In fiery heats I fry,
Yet none approach to warm their hearts
    Or feel my fire, but I.

My faultless breast the furnace is,
    The fuel wounding thorns:
Love is the fire, and sighs the smoke,
    The ashes, shames, and scorns;

The fuel Justice layeth on,
    And mercy blows the coals,
The metal in this furnace wrought,
    Are men's defiled souls:

For which, as now on fire I am,
    To work them to their good,
So will I melt into a bath,
    To wash them in my blood.

With this he vanished out of sight,
    And swiftly shrunk away,
And straight I called unto mind,
    That it was Christmas day.

*Robert Southwell, S.J.*
*(1561-1595)*

# Cradle Song for the Child Jesus

*Ro, ro, ro,*
Our God and Savior,
Do not weep, because You grieve
The Maid who bore You!
*Ro, ro, ro.*

Child, Son of God the Father,
Father of all creation,
Hold back Your tears;
Then Your mother will not grieve,
Since she bore You without pain.
*Ro, ro, ro,*
Give her not Your sorrows, no!

Now, Child, *ro, ro, ro!*
Our God and Savior,
Do not weep, because You grieve
The Maid who bore You!
*Ro, ro, ro.*

> *Gil Vicente*
> *(1465-1540)*

# "Shepherd, shepherd, look who's calling"

*Shepherd, shepherd, look who's calling?*
*"Angels they are, and Day is dawning."*

A solemn chanting I have heard;
It seemed a cantilena.
Look, Bras, since the day is here
Let's seek out the shepherd girl!

*Shepherd, shepherd, look who's calling?*
*"Angels they are, and Day is dawning."*

Who could this youthful Maiden be,
The daughter of the village mayor?
"She is the daughter of God the Father,
And she glimmers like a star."

*Shepherd, shepherd, look who's calling?*
*"Angels they are, and Day is dawning."*

*St. Teresa of Jesus*
*(1515-1582)*

# The Nativity of our Lord and Saviour Jesus Christ

Where is this stupendous stranger,
    Swains of Solyma, advise,
Lead me to my Master's manger,
    Show me where my Saviour lies?

O most Mighty!  O most Holy!
    Far beyond the seraph's thought,
Art thou then so mean and lowly
    As unheeded prophets taught?

O magnitude of meekness!
    Worth from worth immortal sprung;
O the strength of infant weakness,
    If eternal is so young!

Nature's decorations glisten
    Far above their usual trim;
Birds on box and laurels listen,
    As so near the cherubs hymn.

Boreas now no longer winters
    On the desolated coast;
Oaks no more are riv'n in splinters
    By the whirlwind and his host.

Spinks and ouzles sing sublimely,
    'We too have a Saviour born,'
Whiter blossoms burst untimely
    On the blest Mosaic thorn.

God all-bounteous, all-creative,
    Whom no ills from good dissuade,
Is incarnate, and a native
    Of the very world he made.

*Christopher Smart*
*(1722-1771)*

# Christ's Nativity

Awake, glad heart! get up and Sing,
It is the Birth-day of thy King,
    Awake! awake!
    The Sun doth shake
Light from his Locks, and all the way
Breathing Perfumes, doth spice the day.

Awake! awake! heark, how th'wood rings
Winds whisper, and the busy springs
    A Consort make;
    Awake! awake!
Man is their high-priest, and should rise
To offer up the sacrifice.

I would I were some Bird, or Star,
Flutt'ring in woods, or lifted far
    Above this Inn
    And Road of Sin!
Then either Star, or Bird, should be
Shining, or singing, still to thee.

I would I had in my best part
Fit rooms for thee! or that my heart
    Were so clean as
    Thy manger was!
But I am all filth, and obscene,
Yet, if Thou wilt, Thou canst make clean.

Sweet Jesu! will then; Let no more
This Leper haunt, and soil thy door,
Cure him, ease him
Or release him!
And let once more by mystic birth
The Lord of Life be born in Earth.

*Henry Vaughan*
*(1621-1695)*

# "A child lay in a little crib"

A child lay in a little crib;
An ox and ass stood by.
There also was a maiden clear
Maria, who bore that infant dear.
      Jesus, my Lord,
He was that little Child.

Angelic choirs sang overhead
With voices sweet and high.
"Glory, praise, and dignity,
Be to God in all eternity"
      Jesus, my Lord,
He was that little Child.

All was soon to shepherds known.
In wonderment they came running
To Bethlehem and found there
To their joy the Infant fair.
      Jesus, my Lord,
He was that little Child.

*Heinrich von Loufenberg*
*(1390-1460)*

# A Christmas Carol

The shepherds went their hasty way,
    And found the lowly stable-shed
Where the Virgin-Mother lay:
    And now they checked their eager tread,
For to the Babe, that at her bosom clung,
A Mother's song the Virgin-Mother sung.

II

They told her how a glorious light,
    Streaming from a heavenly throng,
Around them shone, suspending night!
    While sweeter than a mother's song,
Blest Angels heralded the Savior's birth,
Glory to God on high! and Peace on Earth.

III

She listened to the tale divine,
    And closer still the Babe she pressed;
And while she cried, the Babe is mine!
    The milk rushed faster to her breast:
Joy rose within her, like a summer's morn;
Peace, Peace on Earth! The Prince of Peace is born.

*Samuel Taylor Coleridge*
*(1772-1834)*

*from*
# On the Morning of Christ's Nativity

## I

It was the Winter wild,
While the Heav'n-born child,
  All meanly wrapt in the rude manger lies;
Nature in awe to him
Had doff't her gaudy trim,
  With her great Master so to sympathize:
It was no season then for her
To wanton with the Sun, her lusty Paramour.

## II

Only with speeches fair
She woos the gentle Air
  To hide her guilty front with innocent Snow,
And on her naked shame,
Pollute with sinful blame,
  The Saintly Veil of Maiden white to throw,
Confounded, that her Maker's eyes
Should look so near upon her foul deformities.

## III

But he her fears to cease
Sent down the meek-ey'd Peace;
  She crowned with Olive green, came softly sliding
Down through the turning sphere,
His ready Harbinger,
  With Turtle wing the amorous clouds dividing,
And waving wide her myrtle wand,
She strikes a universal Peace through Sea and Land.

IV

No War, or Battle's sound
Was heard the World around:
    The idle spear and shield were high up hung;
The hooked Chariot stood
Unstain'd with hostile blood,
    The Trumpet spake not to the armed throng,
And Kings sat still with awful eye,
As if they surely knew their sovran Lord was by.

V

But peaceful was the night
Wherein the Prince of light
    His reign of peace upon the earth began:
The Winds with wonder whist,
Smoothly the waters kiss't,
    Whispering new joys to the mild Ocean,
Who now hath quite forgot to rave,
While Birds of Calm sit brooding on the charmed wave.

*John Milton*
*(1606-1674)*

# "The sky is black, the earth is white"

The sky is black, the earth is white.
O bells, ring out in resonance!
Jesus is born! Towards Him the Virgin
Turns her blessed countenance.

Here no festooned tapestries
Guard the child from drafty cold.
Nought but tattered cobwebs
Drift down from roofbeams old.

He shivers on the fresh-cut straw,
This little infant Jesus dear.
The ox and ass breathe over Him
To warm Him in the manger here.

The thatched eaves bend beneath the snow,
But overhead the skies revel,
And choirs of angels, all in white,
Sing to shepherds, "Noël, Noël!"

*Théophile Gautier*
*(1811-1872)*

# Christmas

The inn is full already; God's Son lies in the hay—
O that my soul could enter there and watch the night!
Come, earthly men, with earthly thought and sight,
Boundless grace you win; in this straw there weeps today
Who would ever weep for us; it were an idle pleasantry
To reverence a kingly cradle filled with straw.
In this crib there lies what the faithful longed to see
Who fulfills the Ages and shall our grief withdraw.

God lies there in our flesh; God, fatherless on earth,
God, motherless in His Divinity; the Co-Creative Word;
God, Father of the maid who conceived and gave Him birth,

And lies now at her feet. Here lies . . . But be spurred
My soul, no longer to rhyme your rough-hewn praise:
The fittest speech is but the silence of a humble gaze.

*Constantijn Huygens*
*(1596-1687)*

# "Welcome, all wonders in one sight"

Welcome, all wonders in one sight!
    Eternity shut in a span,
Summer in winter, day in night,
    Heaven in Earth, and God in man;
Great little one! whose all embracing birth
Lifts earth to heaven, stoops heaven to earth.

Welcome, though not to gold, nor silk,
    To more than Caesar's birthright is;
Two Sister-Seas of Virgin Milk,
    With many a rarely tempered Kiss
That breathes at once both Maid and Mother,
Warms in the one, cools in the other.

She sings thy tears asleep, and dips
    Her Kisses in thy weeping eye,
She spreads the red leaves of thy lips,
    That in their buds yet blushing lie.
She 'gainst those Mother-Diamonds tries
The points of her young Eagle's eyes.

Welcome, though not to those gay flies
    Guilded i'th'beams of earthly Kings,
Slippery souls in smiling eyes,
    But to poor shepherds, home-spun things,
Whose wealth's their flock; whose wit to be
Well read in their simplicity.

Yet when young April's husband showers
    Shall bless the fruitful Maia's bed,
We'll bring the first-born of her flowers,
    To kiss thy feet and crown thy head.
To thee dread Lamb! whose love must keep
The shepherds more than they the sheep.

To Thee, meek Majesty! soft King,
    Of simple Graces and sweet Loves,
Each of us his Lamb will bring,
    Each his pair of Silver Doves,
Till burnt at last in fire of thy fair eyes,
Our selves become our own best sacrifice.

*Richard Crashaw (1612-1649)*
*from "In the Holy Nativity*
*of Our Lord God"*

# A Christmas Carol

In the bleak mid-winter
    Frosty wind made moan,
Earth stood hard as iron,
    Water like a stone;
Snow had fallen, snow on snow,
    Snow on snow,
In the bleak mid-winter
    Long ago.

Our God, Heaven cannot hold Him,
    Nor earth sustain;
Heaven and earth shall flee away
    When He comes to reign:
In the bleak mid-winter
    A stable-place sufficed
The Lord God Almighty
    Jesus Christ.

Enough for Him, whom cherubim
    Worship night and day,
A breast full of milk
    And a manger full of hay;
Enough for Him, whom angels
    Fall down before,
The ox and ass and camel
    Which adore.

Angels and archangels
    May have gathered there,
Cherubim and seraphim
    Thronged the air;

But only His mother
In her maiden bliss
Worshiped the Beloved
With a kiss.

What can I give Him,
Poor as I am?
If I were a shepherd
I would bring a lamb;
If I were a Wise Man,
I would do my part—
Yet what I can I give Him,
Give my heart.

*Christina Rossetti*
*(1830-1894)*

# At the Birth of Christ Our Lord

Today from the Aurora's bosom
A bloom has fallen—a crimson blossom;
And oh, how glorious rests the hay
On which the fallen blossom lay!

When silence gently had unfurled
Her mantle over all below,
And crowned with winter's frost and snow,
Night swayed the scepter of the world.
Amid the gloom descending slow
Upon the earth's ice-fettered bosom,
A bloom has fallen—a crimson blossom.

The only flower the Virgin bore,
Fair as the dawn within her breast,
She gave to earth, yet still possessed
Her virgin blossom as before;
The hay that bright-hued leaf caressed—
Received upon its faithful bosom
That single flower—a crimson blossom.

The manger into which was given,
Amid the wintry snows and cold,
Within its fostering arms to fold
That blushing flower which fell from heaven,
Was as a canopy of gold—
A downy couch—where on its bosom
That bloom had fallen—that crimson blossom.

*Luis de Gongora y Argote* (1561-1627)
*(based on a translation by H. W. Longfellow)*

# New Prince, New Pomp

Behold a silly tender Babe
    In freezing winter night
In homely manger trembling lies:
    Alas a piteous sight!

The Inns are full, no man will yield
    This little Pilgrim bed;
But forced he is with silly beasts
    In crib to shroud his head.

Despise not him for lying there;
    First what he is enquire:
An orient pearl is often found,
    In depth of dirty mire.

Weigh not his crib, his wooden dish,
    Nor beasts that by him feed:
Weigh not his mother's poor attire,
    Nor Joseph's simple weed.

This stable is a Prince's Court,
    The Crib his Chair of State:
The beasts are parcel of his pomp,
    The wooden dish his plate.

The persons in that poor attire,
    His royal liveries wear;
The Prince himself is come from heaven,
    This pomp is prized there.

With joy approach, O Christian wight,
    Do homage to thy King;
And highly praise this humble pomp,
    Which he from heaven doth bring.

*Robert Southwell, S.J.*
*(1561-1595)*

## "In dulci jubilo"

In dulci jubilo
Let us our homage show.
Our heart's joy reclineth
In praesepio,
And like a bright star shineth
Matris in gremio
Qui Alpha es et O,
Qui Alpha es et O.

O Jesu parvule
I yearn for thee alway!
Hear me, I beseech thee,
O puer optime!
My prayer let it reach thee.
Princeps gloriae
Trahe me post te,
Trahe me post te!

O patris caritas!
O Nati lenitas!
Deeply were we stained
Per nostra crimina.
But thou hast for us gained
Coelorum gaudia.
O that we were there!
O that we were there!

*Ubi sunt gaudia,*
If that they be not there?
There are angels singing
*Nova cantica.*
And there the bells are ringing
*In regis curia.*
O that we were there!
O that we were there!

*Henry Suso, O.P. (1300-1366)*
*trans. R. L. Pearsall (1795-1856)*

# Ballad for the Day of Christmas

Now Christmas has danced its round again!
Let's to the fields, my pretty maids!
Let's all take baskets, bowls, and sacks,
Blow flutes and pipes and bleating horns!
For now's no time to clamp our beaks!
Let's sing and leap and prance in rings!
Let's visit the Child in His poor nest,
Whom Elias, and even Enoch, praised,
Who was worshipped by many dukes and kings
(So we'll go too, and take a look!)
*Sing Noël, from eve to dawn's bright nook!*

Colin Georget and, you, Margot du Clak!
Listen to me and don't go nodding off!
Not long ago when by a pond I napped,
I saw on a roadway wide and dusty
An Infant Child who grappled with
A monstrous snake! a poisonous asp!
This plucky Kid, before I knew it,
Whacked it with a Cross so big and hard
He knocked it down and broke its back
(It couldn't squeak, it was so shook!)
*Sing Noël, from eve to dawn's bright nook!*

As I saw him smacking it (with wham and bam!)
And handing it so marvelous a beating,
I heard from high an angel speak:
"Sing Noël (no matter if in French or Greek!)
Don't give a fig for grief or sorrow!
The serpent's age-old power is snapped!"

I blinked and woke, all in a dither,
Crammed my sheep beneath a crag,
And gallantly as any arch-duke can,
To Bethlehem I ran! Robin, Gauthier, and Rook!
*Sing Noël, from eve to dawn's bright nook!*

*Envoi*

Pious Prince, most Catholic King,
His stable's not made of stone or brick,
For winds burst through it in gusts so thick.
(That this is so, just ask St. Luke!)
Let's go now; let sorrow dangle from a hook!
*Sing Noël, from eve to dawn's bright nook!*

*Clement Marot*
*(1495-1544)*

# A Short Christmas Poem of the Ox
# and the Ass at the Crib

The wind over lonely streets
    Stretches out its frozen wing,
Into the crib at Bethlehem
    It blows fierce and howling.
This herald of the wintry cold
    Roars throughout the land;
It grips hard the tender limbs
    Of the newly God-made-man.

But O, let up your howling gusts,
    O boisterous wind, forbear!
Let up your ice-cold blustering,
    This beautiful Child to spare.
Go thrash your scornful wings
    On the wilderness of the sea;
There you may bluster as you will!
    Let our sleeping Infant be!

In your ears I'd whisper now,
    To you, O Joseph mine:
Mingle hay with fine red roses
    As fodder for ass and kine;
Make for your pious animals
    A balsam of herbs to eat—
Quickly, quickly, lose no time!—
    Give them a breath so sweet.

Then both of you may start to blow
    A fragrant breeze so mild—
O ox and ass in reverence—
    To warm this little Child.
O breathe and blow and puff:
    Huff, huff, huff;
Exhale your hearty cheeks so rough:
    Huff, huff, huff!

*Friedrich von Spee, S.J.*
*(1591-1635)*

# "Such great joy I feel!"
(in two voices)

Such great joy I feel!
   Huy ho!
     *"I feel it too, indeed!*
       *Huy ha!"*
For He who made us
Was born to save us,
       *"Huy ha!"*
   Huy ho!
    The night that He was born!

In the very deep of night
When all was hushed and silent,
To shed light upon our souls
A lucid star was born for us,
The lucid star of Jacob.
   Huy ho!
     *"Let's all rejoice, aha!*
       *Huy ha"!*
For He who made us
Was born to save us,
       *"Huy ha!"*
   Huy ho!
    The night that He was born!

In Bethlehem, our home,
A stunning brilliance shone;
This little town, I tell you,
Shall blossom through the world,
For it bore such blessed fruit.
   Huy ho!
     *"Great honor will be given it!*
       *Huy ha!"*

For He who made us
Was born to save us,
> *"Huy ha!"*

 Huy ho!
  The night that He was born!

A Virgin of but fifteen years,
Dusky-skinned, such festive eyes:
Such a comely shepherdess
You'd find not in a thousand flocks!
This sight was never seen before!
 Huy ho!
> *"Never was and never shall again!*
> *Huy ha!"*

For He who made us
Was born to save us,
> *"Huy ha!"*

 Huy ho!
  The night that He was born!

The morning is astir and fresh!
Let's hurry, for now it's day!
Let's search for Mary,
The daughter of Saint Anna,
For she (yes, she!) gave birth to Him!
 Huy ho!
> *"Let's go! Let's go! Come on, let's go!*
> *Huy ha!"*

For He who made us
Was born to save us,
> *"Huy ha!"*

 Huy ho!
  The night that He was born!

*Juan del Encina* (1468-1530)
*from "Egloga de Navidad"*

# Little Song of the Virgin

For you walk among the palms,
O sacred angels,
*That my Child would sleep—*
*Hold back the branches.*

O Palms of Bethlehem
Whom the tumultuous winds
Stir to such a tempest
And gusting yet so strong:
Make less commotion,
Nor flurry at a swifter pace.
*That my Child would sleep—*
*Hold back the branches.*

The Divine Child,
Is wearied now
With weeping on this earth.
To find repose,
He seeks but a pause
Amidst His tender plaint.
*That my Child would sleep—*
*Hold back the branches.*

Rigorous frosts
Encompass Him on every side.
You see I do not have
A way to guard His warmth.
O sacred angels,
Who depart in flight,
*That my Child would sleep—*
*Hold back the branches.*

*Lope de Vega*
*(1562-1635)*

# On the Nativity

The time now having finally come
When his birth was due,
Like a husband newly wed
From his chamber he withdrew

Embracing his beloved spouse
With outstretched arms so deep.
Him the gracious mother then
In a manger lay to sleep,

Amid the stable's animals
Who there resided at their ease.
Men entoned their canticles
Angels sang their melodies,

Rejoicing in the wedding feast
Of two such spouses side by side.
But God as tiny infant now
In the manger wept and cried.

Tears were the only bridal gems
To adorn this espousal strange.
The mother watched in wonderment
To see such marvelous exchange:

For God was bound to human grief;
In humans boundless joy had grown,
Which to one and to the other
Before this time was never known.

*St. John of the Cross*
*(1542-1591)*

# A Christmas Hymn

*And some of the Pharisees from among*
*the multitude said unto him, Master,*
*rebuke thy disciples.*

*And he answered and said unto them,*
*I tell you that if these should hold their peace,*
*the stones would immediately cry out.*

Luke 19:39-40

A stable lamp is lighted
Whose glow shall wake the sky;
And stars shall bend their voices,
And every stone shall cry.
And every stone shall cry,
And straw like gold shall shine;
A barn shall harbour heaven,
A stall become a shrine.

This child through David's city
Shall ride in triumph by;
The palm shall strew its branches,
And every stone shall cry.
And every stone shall cry,
Though heavy, dull and dumb,
And lie within the roadway
To pave his kingdom come.

Yet he shall be forsaken,
And yielded up to die;
The sky shall groan and darken,
And every stone shall cry.
And every stone shall cry,
For stony hearts of men:
God's blood upon the spearhead,
God's love refused again.

But now, as at the ending,
The low is lifted high;
The stars shall bend their voices,
And every stone shall cry.
And every stone shall cry,
In praises of the child
By whose descent among us
The worlds are reconciled.

*Richard Wilbur*
*(b. 1921)*

# Christmas

The Shepherds sing; and shall I silent be?
    My God, no hymn for thee?

My soul's a shepherd too; a flock it feeds
    Of thoughts and words and deeds.

The Pasture is thy word: the streams, thy grace
    Enriching all the place.

Shepherd and flock shall sing, and all my powers
    Out-sing the daylight hours.

Then we will chide the sun for letting night
    Take up his place and right.

We sing one common Lord: wherefore he should
    Himself the candle hold.

I will go searching till I find a sun
    Shall stay, till we have done:

A willing shiner, that shall shine as gladly
    As frost-nipped suns look sadly.

Then we shall sing, and shine all our own day,
    And one another pay.

His beams shall cheer my breast: and both so twine
    Till even his beams sing, and my music shine.

*George Herbert*
*(1593-1633)*

## "Sweet is she and gently sworn"

Sweet is she and gently sworn
Whom the angel's happy greeting
Swells in heart with love unborn,
God with gracious maiden meeting:
In that perfect welcoming,
Heaven, earth, and angel sing.

Now she holds him to her breast
Maid a mother's watch is keeping
Over him who is her rest—
God in grateful arms lies sleeping:
Mary's child, of all things king,
Heaven, earth, and angel sing.

*Montague Brown*
*(b. 1952)*

# A Child, My Choice

Let folly praise that fancy loves,
    I praise and love that child
Whose heart, no thought; whose tongue, no word;
    Whose hand no deed defiled.

I praise him most, I love him best,
    All praise and love is his:
While him I love, in him I live,
    And cannot live amiss.

Love's sweetest mark, laud's highest theme,
    Man's most desired light:
To love him, life; to leave him, death;
    To live in him, delight.

He mine, by gift, I his, by debt:
    Thus each, to other due:
First friend he was: best friend he is:
    All times will try him true.

Though young, yet wise; though small, yet strong;
    Though Man, yet God he is:
As wise, he knows; as strong, he can;
    As God, he loves to bliss.

His knowledge rules, his strength defends;
    His love doth cherish all.
His birth, our joy; his life, our light;
    His death, our end of thrall.

Alas, he weeps, he sighs, he pants,
　　Yet do his angels sing;
Out of his tears, his sighs and throbs,
　　Doth bud a joyful spring.

Almighty Babe, whose tender arms
　　Can force all foes to fly;
Correct my faults, protect my life,
　　Direct me when I die.

*Robert Southwell, S.J.*
*(1561-1595)*

# A Christmas Carol

The Christ-child lay on Mary's lap,
    His hair was like a light.
(O weary, weary were the world,
    But here is all aright.)

The Christ-child lay on Mary's breast,
    His hair was like a star.
(O stern and cunning are the kings,
    But here the true hearts are.)

The Christ-child lay on Mary's heart,
    His hair was like a fire.
(O weary, weary is the world,
    But here the world's desire.)

The Christ-child stood at Mary's knee,
    His hair was like a crown,
And all the flowers looked up at Him,
    And all the stars looked down.

*G. K. Chesterton*
*(1874-1936)*

## "O, like a tiny cradle"

*Ach, konnte nur dein Herz*
*zu einer Krippe werden,*
*Gott wurde noch einmal*
*ein Kind auf diesen Erden.*

O, like a tiny cradle,
Could thy heart become,
God would on earth again
Be born an infant son.

*Angelus Silesius*
*(1624-1677)*

# "My mouth will utter the praise of the Lord"

My mouth will utter the praise of the Lord,
of the Lord through whom all things have been made
And who has been made amidst all things;

Who is the Revealer of His Father, Creator of His mother;
who is the Son of God from His Father without a mother,
The Son of Man through His mother without a father.

He is as great as the Day of the Angels,
and as small as a day in the life of men;
He is the Word of God before all ages,
and the Word made flesh at the destined time.

Maker of the sun, He is made beneath the sun.
Disposing all the ages from the bosom of the Father,
He consecrates this very day in the womb of His mother.
In His Father He abides; from His mother He goes forth.

Creator of heaven and earth,
under the heavens He was born upon earth.
Wise beyond all speech, as a speechless child He is wise.
Filling the whole world, He lies in a manger.
Ruling the stars, He nurses at His mother's breast.

He is great in the form of God
and small in the form of a servant,
So much so that His greatness
is not diminished by His smallness,
Nor His smallness concealed by His greatness.

For when He assumed a human body,
    He did not forsake divine works.
He did not cease to be concerned mightily
    from one end of the universe to the other,
And to order all things delightfully, when,
    having clothed Himself in the fragility of the flesh,
He was received into, not confined in,
    the Virgin's womb.

So that, while the food of wisdom
    was not taken away from the angels,
We were to taste how sweet is the Lord.

*St. Augustine* *(354-430)*
*Sermo in Natale Domini IV*

*Praise the Lord from the heavens,*
*Praise Him in the heights!*
*Praise Him, all you angels;*
*Praise Him, all you heavenly array.*
*Praise Him, sun and moon;*
*Praise Him all you shining stars.*

*Let them praise the name of the Lord,*
*For He spoke and they were created.*
*He has established them forever and ever:*
*He has affixed boundaries for them*
*That they shall never overreach.*

*Praise the Lord from the earth,*
*All you whales and depths of the sea,*
*All fire and hail, all snow and mist,*
*All stormy winds that do His bidding;*
*All you mountains and hills,*
*Orchards and forests, beasts and cattle,*
*Serpents on the earth and birds in the air.*

*Let kings of the earth and all peoples,*
*Princes and judges, men and maidens,*
*Old and young, praise the name of the Lord,*

*For His name alone is exalted;*
*His majesty is above heaven and earth.*
*He has raised the Horn of His chosen ones;*
*May His faithful, the seed of Israel,*
*And those who are dear to Him,*
*Give Him honor and praise forever.*

Psalm 148

PART IV

# BRIGHT STAR OF JACOB

A STAR SHALL ARISE FROM JACOB
AND FROM THE ROOTS OF ISRAEL
SHALL SPRING A ROYAL SCEPTER.

Numbers 24:17

*He shall be like rain on the fleece,*
*like showers on the earth.*
*Justice and peace shall bloom*
*in His days.*

*He shall rule from sea to sea,*
*and from the River of Oceans*
*to the ends of the earth.*
*The kings of Tharsis and the Islands*
*shall bring tribute;*
*the kings of Arabia and Saba*
*shall offer gifts.*

*Grain fields shall flourish*
*to the tops of the mountains;*
*they shall rustle in the wind*
*like the forests of Lebanon;*
*and the city dwellers shall blossom*
*like the fruit of the fields.*

*May His name be blessed forever;*
*in Him all the nations of the earth*
*shall be blessed.*

Psalm 72:6-8, 10, 16-17

*And the star*
*that they had seen at its rising*
*went before them, until it came and stood over*
*the place where the child was.*

*They greatly rejoiced*
*when they saw that the star stood still.*
*Entering the house and finding the child*
*with Mary His mother,*
*they knelt down*
*and worshipped Him.*

*And opening their treasures*
*they offered Him gifts*
*of gold, frankincense, and myrrh.*

Matthew 2:9-11

# "It all happened beneath
the clearness of the skies"

*Tout cela se passait sous la clarté des cieux:*
*Les anges dans la nuit avaient formé des choeurs.*
*Les anges dans la nuit chantaient comme des fleurs.*
*Par dessus les bergers, par dessus les rois mages*
*Les anges dans la nuit chantaient éternellement.*

It all happened beneath the clearness of the skies—
The angels in the night had assembled into choirs,
The angels in the night sang like flowers.
Far above the shepherds, far above the Magian Kings,
The angels in the night sang eternally.

Under the goodness, under the youth,
    under the eternity of the skies,
Of the firmament which is called heaven!
Like the flowers of song, like the flowers of hymns,
    like the flowers of prayer, like the flowers
        of the action of grace
Like a flourishing, like a foundation,
    like a fructification of prayer and grace.

All that happened under the choirs of angels,
All that happened under the goodness of the skies—
The star shone in the night like a point of gold,
The star shone in the night eternally,
The star shone in the night like a pinnacle of gold.

*Charles Peguy (1873-1914)*
*from Le Mystère de la Charité de Jeanne D'Arc*

# "Him who dwells beyond the worlds"

Him who dwells beyond the worlds
    The Virgin bore today.
Him who bounds the universe,
    Earth shelters in a cave.
Angels above the shepherds high
    Sing His bounteous praise.
Wise Men, guided by a star,
    Pursue their eager way.
*For unto us is born,*
    *A tiny child, God of Eternal Aeons.*

Bethlehem blooms as Eden, now,
    Come, let us go and see.
In a hidden covert there,
    We'll find all pleasantry.
Deep inside that stony cave,
    Paradise itself shall be.
For there the bud of kindliness
    Has burst the arid waste.
For there a well has sprung
    Which David longed to taste
For there a Virgin bears a child
    Who Adam's thirst shall sate.
*For unto us is born,*
    *A tiny child, God of Eternal Aeons.*

*St. Romanos*
*(c. 540)*

# "Three Holy Kings from the Orient"

Three Holy Kings from the Orient
    In town after town did appear:
"O where is the way to Bethlehem,
    You maidens and lads so dear?"

Neither the young nor the old could say;
    The Kings traveled farther on.
They followed a pure and golden star
    That brightly glittered from far.

Over Joseph's house the star stood still,
    The Three Holy Kings entered in;
The oxen lowed, the little Child cried
    And the Kings began to sing.

*Heinrich Heine*
*(1797-1856)*

# The Star-Song:
## A Caroll to the King,
## Sung at White Hall

*First:*
>Tell us, thou clear and heavenly Tongue,
>Where is the Babe but lately sprung?
>Lies He the Lilly-banks among?

*Second:*
>Or say, if this new Birth of ours
>Sleeps, laid within some Ark of Flowers,
>Spangled with dew-light; thou canst clear
>All doubts, and manifest the where.

*Third:*
>Declare to us, bright Star, if we shall seek
>Him in the Morning's blushing cheek,
>Or search the beds of Spices through,
>To find him out?

*Star:*
>No, this ye need not do;
>But only come and see Him rest
>A Princely Babe in's Mother's Breast

*Chorus:*
>He's seen, He's seen, why then a Round,
>Let's kiss the sweet and holy ground;
>And all rejoice that we have found
>*A King, before conception crowned.*

*Fourth:*
>Come then, come then, and let us bring
>Unto our pretty *Twelfth-Tide King,*
>Each one his several offering;

*Chorus:*
>And when night comes, we'll give Him wassailing
>And that His treble Honours may be seen,
>We'll chose Him King, and make His Mother Queen.

>*Robert Herrick*
>*(1591-1674)*

# "Lord when the wise men came from far"

Lord when the wise men came from far,
Led to thy Cradle by a Star,
Then did the shepherds too rejoice,
Instructed by the angels' voice:
Blest were the wise men in their skill,
And shepherds in their harmless will.

Wise men in tracing nature's laws
Ascend unto the highest cause,
Shepherds with humble fearfulness
Walk safely, though their light be less:
Though wise men better know the way,
It seems no honest heart can stray.

There is no merit in the wise
But love, (the shepherds' sacrifice).
Wise men all ways of knowledge past,
To the shepherds' wonder come at last:
To know can only wonder breed,
And not to know is wonder's seed.

A wise man at the altar bows
And offers up his studied vows
And is received; may not the tears,
Which spring too from a shepherd's fears,
And sighs upon his frailty spent,
Though not distinct, be eloquent?

'Tis true, the object sanctifies
All passions which within us rise,
And since no creature comprehends
The cause of causes, end of ends,
He who himself vouchsafes to know
Best pleases his Creator so.

When then our sorrows we apply
To our own wants and poverty,
When we look up in all distress
And our own misery confess,
Sending both thanks and prayers above,
Then though we do not know, we love.

*Sidney Godolphin*
*(1610-1643)*

# "Rod of the Root of Jesse"

Rod of the Root of Jesse,
    Thou, Blossom of Mary born,
From that thick shady mountain,
    Cam'st glorious forth this morn:
Of her, the Ever-Virgin,
    Incarnate wast Thou made,
The immaterial Essence,
    The God by all obeyed!

In Balaam's ancient vision
    The Eastern seers were skilled;
They traced the constellations,
    And joy their spirits filled:
For Thou, bright Star of Jacob,
    Ascending in Thy might,
Summoned these first Gentiles here
    To worship in Thy light.

As on a fleece descending
    The gentle dews distil,
As rain o'erflows the cistern
    The Virgin didst Thou fill.
Tarshish and Ethiopia,
    The Isles and Araby,
And Media, leagued with Sheba,
    Fall down and worship Thee.

*St. Cosmas (d. 760)*
*Trans. by J. M. Neale*

# Epiphany

Balthazar, Melchior, and Gaspar, those Magian Kings,
Laden with coffers of silver and rose-gilt enameling
And followed by long, long caravans of camels,
Press forward, just as fine old paintings show.

From the distant Orient, they bear their homage
To the feet of the Son of God, born to heal the woes
Which both men and animals suffer here below.
A black page upholds their embroidered robes.

On the stable threshold, where Joseph keeps his watch,
They lift their crowns most modestly from royal heads
To greet the Child who laughs at them in wonder.

It was like this, in days of old, under Augustus Caesar,
That they came, offering their gold, incense, and myrrh,
Those star-gazing Kings, Gaspar, Melchior, and Balthazar.

*José-Maria de Heredia*
*(1842-1905)*

# Christmas Star

It was winter.
The wind blew from the steppes.
The child was cold
In the grotto on the slope of a hill.

The breath of an ox comforted him.
Calves and sheep
Crowded together in the cave.
A warm mist hung over the manger.

At midnight on a stony outcrop,
Shepherds shook chaff from their shaggy capes
And grains from their straw bedding.
They looked drowsily into the distance.

Far off were fields and fences,
And village headstones covered with snow,
And cart-shafts deep in a snow drift.
Above the headstones, the sky was full of stars.

Among them, unseen until now,
More dimly lit than an oil lamp
Hung in a watchman's window,
A Star shone on the road to Bethlehem.

It rose in the sky like a haystack aflame,
Of fiery straw and thatch.
All creation shuddered in awe,
Astonished by this new Star.

Its scarlet nimbus grew wider and deeper—
A portent for all to see;
Three stargazers saw the blaze from afar;
They hurried after its beckoning light.

Their camels were laden with gifts.
Their saddled donkeys, sure-footed and tiny,
Trod in little steps down the hills.

In the misty dawn, as gray as ash,
Draymen and shepherds stamped their feet.
Footmen squabbled with horsemen.
By a water-trough in a hollowed log,
Camels bellowed and asses brayed.

There was light. Dawn swept the final stars
From heaven's arch like specks of ash.
From the teeming rabble, the Magi alone
Mary allowed to enter the hillside grotto.

He slept in the oaken manger, aglow with light,
Like a moonbeam in the cleft of a tree.
The warm breath from an ox and an ass
Enveloped him, as if in a sheepskin robe.

The Magi stood in the shadowy den;
They whispered in stammering words.
Suddenly, from the dark, they were nudged
To move a little aside from the manger;
They looked around; like a guest at the threshold,
The Christmas Star gazed upon the Maid.

*Boris Pasternak*
*(1890-1960)*

# On the Feast of the Holy Three Kings

Through the night three wanderers go:
Their brows are bound by purple bands;
Their skins are burned by scorching winds
And toilsome ways through desert lands.
Past the palm trees' rustling green,
The servants follow far behind.
Golden tassels and tinkling bells
Slung from the camels' saddle-seats
Jangle as they travel forward,
While coffers waft aromas sweet.

Darkness holds them black and dense,
Hiding all the landscape near;
Looming shadows threaten them.
Wanderers, then, did you not fear?
Despite a thousand misty veils
That hung across the silent moors,
Steadfast through the tender dusk
A tiny star shone sparkling bright,
Gently gliding in deepest blue.
The caravan pursued its light.

Listen, how the servants murmur!
"When will some fine town appear
With verdant groves and temples high?
See, how our woes will persevere!
Whether the waste is burning hot
And vipers coil around our feet,
And tigers crouch along our path
And fiery winds our faces singe:
White ovals, glimmering in the dark,
Eye the gifts meant for the King."

Other matters of deep impress
Draw the three across the night;
Like silent moons the three advance
Aglow in starry solar-light.
When avalanches thunder down,
When with gigantic petals bright
Flowers streak the desert waste,
They fix their steady gaze from far
Upon that Power which lures them on
And kindled that miraculous star.

*Annette von Droste-Hülsoff*
*(1797-1848)*

# Journey of the Magi

'A cold coming we had of it,
Just the worst time of the year
For a journey, and such a long journey:
The ways deep and the weather sharp,
The very dead of winter.'
And the camels galled, sore-footed, refractory,
Lying down in the melting snow.
There were times we regretted
The summer palaces on slopes, the terraces,
And the silken girls bringing sherbet.
Then the camel men cursing and grumbling
And running away, and wanting their liquor and women,
And the night-fires going out, and the lack of shelters,
And the cities hostile and the towns unfriendly
And the villages dirty and charging high prices:
A hard time we had of it.
At the end we preferred to travel all night,
Sleeping in snatches,
With the voices singing in our ears, saying
That this was all folly.

Then at dawn we came down to a temperate valley,
Wet, below the snow line, smelling of vegetation;
With a running stream and a water-mill beating the darkness,
And three trees on the low sky,
And an old white horse galloped away in the meadow.
Then we came to a tavern with vine-leaves over the lintel,
Six hands at an open door dicing for pieces of silver,
And feet kicking the empty wine-skins.
But there was no information, and so we continued
And arrived at evening, not a moment too soon
Finding the place; it was (you may say) satisfactory.

All this was a long time ago, I remember,
And I would do it again, but set down
This set down
This: were we led all that way for
Birth or Death? There was a Birth, certainly,
We had evidence and no doubt. I had seen birth and death,
But had thought they were different; this Birth was
Hard and bitter agony for us, like Death, our death.
We returned to our places, these Kingdoms,
But no longer at ease here, in the old dispensation,
With an alien people clutching their gods.
I should be glad of another death.

*T. S. Eliot*
*(1888-1965)*

# The Birth of Christ

Had you not simplicity, how should it befall you
What the darkest night illuminates?
Behold how God, who thundered over the nations,
So tenderly through you enters the world.

    Had you imagined something a bit more grand?

What is grandeur? Aslant through all dominions
He traversed, He thrust His measured destiny.
Even a star has no such regal path.
Do you see, these kings themselves are grand:

    To you they trudge, hoarding before your lap

Treasures, which they hold as grandest things;
And maybe you are astonished at these gifts. . . .
But peer into the enfolding of your cloak
How He, already, outshines them all.

    All amber, shipped from distant climes,

Each golden artifact and perfumed spice
That roams distraught among the senses—
All these were of such sudden brevity
And, in the end, brought only sorrow.

    But (you will see) He, alone, brings joy.

*Rainer Maria Rilke*
*(1875-1926)*

# Preface for the Octave of Christmas

It is truly just, necessary and beneficent
to give you thanks, holy Lord, all-powerful Father,
Eternal God, through Jesus Christ our Lord.

In celebrating today the octave of your birth,
we celebrate, O Lord, your marvelous deeds,
because she who has given birth is mother and virgin,
and He who was born is infant and God.

For good reason, the heavens have spoken,
the angels have sung, the shepherds were joyful,
the Magi were transformed, the kings seized with fright,
and infants were crowned with the glory of blood.

Nourish, O mother, Him who is your nourishment.
Nourish the bread descended from heaven
and placed in the manger like the fodder of animals.
The ox saw his Master; the donkey, the crib of his Lord.

He is worthy of circumcision in order to fulfill
all prophecies about Him, our Savior and Lord,
whom Simeon received into the Temple.

Thus let us sing with the angels and the archangels,
with the Thrones and Dominions, with all the choirs
of Heaven, this hymn of glory:

Holy, Holy, Holy, Lord God of Hosts,
Heaven and earth are filled with your glory.
Hosanna in the highest! Blessed is He who comes
in the name of the Lord. Hosanna in the highest!

*Gelasien Sacramentary*
*(c. 500)*

*Now You dismiss Your servant in peace,*
*O Lord, according to your word,*
*because my eyes have seen Your salvation*
*which You have prepared*
*before the countenance*
*of all peoples:*

*A light of revelation unto the nations,*
*and the glory of Your people*
*Israel.*

Luke 2:29-32
*The Song of Simeon*

HE IS THE IMAGE
OF THE INVISIBLE GOD,
THE FIRST BORN
OF EVERY CREATURE.

FOR IN HIM
WERE CREATED
ALL THINGS
IN THE HEAVENS AND ON THE EARTH,
THINGS VISIBLE AND INVISIBLE,
WHETHER THRONES OR DOMINATIONS,
PRINCIPALITIES OR POWERS.

ALL THINGS
HAVE BEEN CREATED
THROUGH HIM AND FOR HIM,
AND HE IS SOVEREIGN OVER ALL THINGS,
AND IN HIM
ALL THINGS
ARE BOUND
TOGETHER.


Colossians 1:15-17

# Appendix A

## Chronological listing of works in this collection

Publius Vergilius Maro (70-19 B.C.): from "The Fourth Eclogue" [Latin—trans. John Dryden (1631-1700); excerpt].

St. Cyril of Jerusalem (315-386): "We do not only proclaim one coming of Christ"—"*Parousian katanggellomen ou mian monon*" [Greek; excerpt from *Katecheses XV*].

Prudentius (348-413): "Born of the Father's Heart"—"*Corde natus ex parentis ante mundi exordium*" [Latin].

St. Augustine (354-430): "My mouth will utter the praise of the Lord"—"*Laudem Domini loquetur os meum*" [Latin; excerpt from "*Sermo in Natale Domini IV*"].

Gelasien Sacramentary (c. 500): "Preface for the Octave of Christmas"—"*Praefatio de Octava Nativitatis Domini*" [Latin].

St. Romanos (c. 540): "Him who dwells beyond the worlds"—"*He parthenos semeron ton huperousian tiktei*" [Greek; excerpt].

Roman Antiphonary (early 600s): "The Advent Antiphons" [Latin].

St. Cosmas (d. 760): "Rod of the Root of Jesse"—"*Rhabdos ek tes rhidzes*" [Greek—trans. J. M. Neale; excerpt].

Cynewulf (c. 800): "*Earendael*" [Anglo-Saxon; excerpt from *The Advent Lyrics*].

St. Bernard of Clairvaux (1090-1153; attributed): "Faithful choir, rejoicing sing"—"*Laetabundus exultet, fidelis chorus*" [Latin; excerpt].

Peter the Venerable (d. 1155): "Heaven rejoice! Earth clap your hands"—
"*Caelum gaude, terra plaude*" [Latin; excerpt].

Advent Processional Hymn (1200s; anonymous): "Gideon's threshing
floor"—"*Gedeonis area, celitus perfusa rore*" [Latin].

St. Bonaventure (1221-1274): "The heavens were made honey sweet"—
"*Melliflui facti sunt caeli*" [Latin; excerpt from *Lignum Vitae*, I, 4].

Dante Alighieri (1265-1321): "Virgin Mother, Daughter of thy Son"—
"*Vergine Madre, figlia del tuo figlio*" [Italian; excerpt from the
*Paradiso*, XXXIII].

Henry Suso, O.P. (1300-1366; attributed): "*In dulci jubilo*" [macaronic Latin-
Middle High German—trans. R. L. Pearsall (1795-1856); excerpt].

Johannes Tauler O.P. (1300-1371; attributed): "There comes a ship so
laden"—"*Es kumpt ein schiff geladen*" [Middle High German; excerpt].

Geoffrey Chaucer (1343-1400): from "*Invocacio ad Mariam*" [Middle
English: Excerpt from "The Prologe of the Seconde Nonnes Tale"
in *The Canterbury Tales*].

Heinrich von Loufenberg (1390-1460): "A child lay in a little crib"—
"*In einem kripfli lag ein kind*" [Middle High German; excerpt].

Anonymous (early 1400s): "I sing of a maiden" [Middle English].

Anonymous (1400s): "*Rosa Mystica*" [macaronic Latin-Middle English].

Gil Vicente (1465-1540): "Cradle Song for the Child Jesus"—"*Cancion de
cuna al niño Jesus*" [Spanish; also a version in Portuguese].

Juan del Encina (1468-1530): "Such great joy I feel!"—"*Gran gasajo siento yo*"
[Spanish; excerpt from *Egloga de Navidad*].

Clement Marot (1495-1544): "Ballad for the Day of Christmas"—"*Ballade
du Jour de Noël*" [French].

Fray Ambrosio Montesino (c. 1500): "No, we must not sleep"—"*No la
debemos dormir*" [Spanish].

Anonymous (1500s): "A spotless Rose is blooming"—"*Es ist ein Ros
entsprungen*" [German—trans. anonymous].

St. Teresa of Jesus (1515-1582): "Shepherd, shepherd, look who's calling"—
"*Mi gallejo, mira quien llama*" [Spanish].

St. John of the Cross (1542-1591): "On the Nativity"—"*Del Nacimiento*"
[Spanish].

Robert Southwell, S.J. (1561-1595): "The Burning Babe"; "New Prince,
New Pomp"; "A Child, My Choice" [English].

Luis de Gongora y Argote (1561-1627): "At the Birth of Christ Our Lord"—
"*Al Nacimiento de Christo Nuestro Señor*" [Spanish—based on a trans-
lation by H. W. Longfellow].

Lope de Vega (1562-1635): "Little Song of the Virgin"—"*Cantarcillo de la
Virgen*" [Spanish].

John Donne (1572-1631): "If some king of the earth"; "Annunciation"
[English; excerpts from "Sermon for Christmas Day 1624" and
from "*La Corona*" respectively].

Ben Jonson (1573-1637): "A Hymn on the Nativity of my Saviour" [English]

Friedrich von Spee, S.J. (1591-1635): "A Short Christmas Poem of the Ox and
the Ass at the Crib"—"*Ein kurz poetisch Christ-Gedicht vom Ochs und
Eselein bei der Krippen*" [German].

Robert Herrick (1591-1674): "The Star-Song: A Caroll to the King, Sung at
White Hall" [English].

George Herbert (1593-1633): "Christmas" [English; excerpt].

Esteban de Zafra (c. 1595): "Underneath this crag is born"—"*Bajo de la
pena nace*" [Spanish].

Constantijn Huygens (1596-1687): "Christmas"—"*Kerstmis*" [Dutch].

John Milton (1608-1674): from "On the Morning of Christ's Nativity"
[English; excerpt].

Sidney Godolphin (1610-1643): "Lord when the wise men came from far"
[English]

Richard Crashaw (1612-1649): "*O Gloriosa Domina*"; "Welcome all wonders
in one sight" [English; a translation from a medieval Latin hymn and
an excerpt from "In the Holy Nativity of Our Lord God"].

Andreas Gryphius (1616-1664): "On the Birth of Jesus"—"*Über der Geburt
Jesu*" [German].

Henry Vaughan (1621-1695): "Christ's Nativity" [English; excerpt].

Angelus Silesius (1624-1677): "O, like a tiny cradle"—"*Ach, konnte nur dein
Herz*" [German].

Laurent Drelincourt (1626-1681): "On the Nativity of Our Lord"—"*Sur la
Naissance de Notre Seigneur*" [French].

Quirinus Kuhlmann (1651-1689): "The Birth Night of the Lord"—"*Die
Geburtsnacht des Herrn*" [German].

Alexander Pope (1688-1744): "A *Virgin* shall conceive, a *Virgin* bear a Son!"
[English; excerpt from "Messiah: A Sacred Eclogue"].

Christopher Smart (1722-1771): "The Nativity of our Lord and Saviour Jesus Christ" [English].

Samuel Taylor Coleridge (1772-1834): "A Christmas Carol" [English; excerpt].

Annette von Droste-Hülsoff (1797-1848): "On the Feast of the Holy Three Kings"—"*Am Feste der hl. drei Könige*" [German; excerpt].

Heinrich Heine (1797-1856): "Three Holy Kings from the Orient"—"*Die heilgen drei Könige aus Morgenland*" [German].

Théophile Gautier (1811-1872): "The sky is black, the earth is white"—"*Le ciel est noir, la terre est blanche*" [French].

Christina Rossetti (1830-1894): "A Christmas Carol" [English].

José-Maria de Heredia (1842-1905): "Epiphany"—"*Épiphanie*" [French].

Gerard Manley Hopkins, S.J. (1844-1889): "Of her flesh He took flesh" [English; excerpt from "The Virgin Mary Compared to the Air We Breathe"].

Oscar Wilde (1854-1900): "*Ave Maria Gratia Plena*" [English].

William Butler Yeats (1865-1939): "The Mother of God" [English].

Paul Claudel (1868-1955): "*Salut,* woman in splendor upon her knees"—"*Salut, femme à genoux dans la splendeur*" [French; excerpt from "*Chant de Marche de Noël*"].

Charles Peguy (1873-1914): "It all happened beneath the clearness of the skies"—"*Tout cela se passait sous la clarté des cieux*" [French; excerpt from *Le Mystère de la Charité de Jeanne D'Arc*].

G. K. Chesterton (1874-1936): "A Child of the Snows"; "A Christmas Carol" [English].

Rainer Maria Rilke (1875-1926): "The Birth of Christ"—"*Geburt Christi*" [German].

T. S. Eliot (1888-1965): "Journey of the Magi" [English].

Gabriela Mistral (1889-1957): "*Yo no tengo soledad*" [Spanish].

Boris Pasternak (1890-1960): "Christmas Star"—"*Rojdestvenskaya Zvezda*" [Russian; excerpt].

Richard Wilbur (b. 1921): "A Christmas Hymn" [English].

Montague Brown (b. 1952): "Sweet is she and gently sworn" [English].

# Appendix B

## Additional poems for further reading

For those interested in pursuing the history of Nativity poems (with some emphasis on the English tradition), the following list of works, organized chronologically, is provided as an addendum to the works already presented in the collection and as a starting point for further research. I would like to have included some of these poems in the collection, but considerations of variety, or appropriateness, or length have, in many cases, precluded the selection. In any case, this list represents but a sampling of a long, complex, and uniquely prolific tradition.

For the large number of anonymous nativity poems, as well as for the Christmas carols that exist in the various European languages, many collections are available and should be consulted. Other sources for Nativity verse are the medieval, Renaissance, and modern Christmas and Epiphany plays that are to be found in the major European literary traditions. Nativity materials may also be explored at length in liturgical works and anthologies of various kinds: for example, the Liturgy of the Hours, the Missals that have developed over the centuries in the Catholic tradition, collections of prayers, hymns, and liturgical services for special feast days to be found in the Christian tradition, including the Orthodox and the Protestant, and sermons by the great orators of the Christian pulpit, many of which contain passages of striking eloquence and beauty.

Especially fecund sources for Nativity materials are the verbal accompaniments for musicological texts, such as motets, oratorios, madrigals, and other kinds of musical compositions. Finally, the Slavic, Scandinavian, Portuguese, and various Levantine literary traditions merit much deeper attention than I have been able to give them.

*Oracula Sibyllina* (c. 200): Book VIII

Juvencus (c. 330): *Evangeliorum Libri Quattuor,* Book I

Hilary of Poitiers (d. 368): "*Jesus refulsit omnium*"

Ephrem the Syrian (d. 373): Hymns on the Nativity

St. Ambrose (340-397): "*Veni, Redemptor gentium*"

Prudentius (348-413): "*Quid est quod artum circulum*"; "*Quicumque Christum quaeritis*"

Synesius of Cyrene (370-414): Hymns V and VII

The Akathistos Hymn (400s)

Sedulius (c. 431): *Carmen Paschale,* Book II; "*A solis ortus cardine*"

St. Anatolius (d. 458): "*En Bethleem gennatai*"

Venantius Fortunatus (530-609): "*Agnoscat omne saeculum*"

Anonymous (late 500s): "*Conditor alme siderum*"

Blathmacc (700s): "*Soera ngein ro génair úait/ rot rath, a Maire, mórbúaid/ Crist macc Dé Athar de nim*"

St. John Damascene (c. 730): "*Henegke gaster hegiasmene Logon*"

Cynewulf (c. 800): "The Advent Lyrics" from *Christ* I.

Walafrid Strabo (808-849): "*Lumen inclytum refulget*"

Notker of St. Gall (840-912): "*Eja, recolamus laudibus piis digna*"

Old Saxon *Heliand* (c. 830), Section V

Otfrid von Weissenburg (c. 868): *Das Evangelienbuch,* Book I: 11, 12, 13, 17

The Blickling Homilies (c. 971): "*Crist se Goldbloma*"

Abelard (1079-1142): "*Verbo Verbum virgo concipiens*"; "*Dei patris et matris unicus*"; "*Quam beatum stratum hoc straminis*"; and other hymns and sequences *in nativitate domini*

Walther von der Vogelweide (1170-1230): "*Mit saelden müese ich hiute uf sten*"; "*Maget und muoter, schouwe der kristenheite not*"

Jacopone da Todi (1228-1306): "A Canticle of the Nativity"; "A Second Canticle of the Nativity"; "*Stabat Mater speciosa*"

Richard Ledrede, O.F.M. (1317-1360): "*Cantilena de nativitate domini,*" "*Alia cantilena de eodem festo,*" and others

John Audelay (c. 1426): "*In die natalis domini*"; "*In die Epephanis*"

Jacapo Sannazaro (1448-1530): *De partu virginis*

James Ryman, O.F.M. (late 1400s): "Upon a night an aungell bright";
   "A sterre shone bright on Twelfthe Day"

William Dunbar (1465-1520): "*Rorate coeli desuper!* Heavens, distill your
   balmy showers"

Gil Vicente (1465-1540): "*Branca estais e colorada / Virgem sagrada,*"
   and others

Desiderius Erasmus (1469-1536): "*De casa natalita pueri Jesu*"

Martin Luther (1483-1546): "*Vom Himmel hoch, da komm ich her*"

Marco Girolamo Vida (1490-1566): *Christiad,* Book III, 541-799.

Clement Marot (1495-1544): "*Une pastourelle gentile*"

Lucrezia Tornabuoni de Medici (early 1500s): "*Ecco 'l Messia, ecco 'l Messia/
   e la madre Maria*"

Vauquelin de la Fresnaye (1535-1607): "*Prenons chacun sa panatière*"

William Byrd (1543-1623): "My sweet little baby, what meanest thou to cry";
   "A Carol for Christmas Day"

Robert Southwell, S.J. (1561-1595): "New Heaven, New War"; "Come to your
   Heaven, you Heavenly choirs"; "The Nativity of Christ"; "The
   Epiphanie"

Richard Verstegan (1565-1620): "Our Lady's Lullaby"

Henry Hawkins, S.J. (1571-1646): "The Bee"

John Donne (1572-1631): "Nativitie," section 3 of "*La Corona*"

Edmund Bolton (1575-1633): "A Carol"

Thomas Pestel (1584-1659): "Psalm for Christmas Day"

William Drummond (1585-1649): "The Angels"

William Austin (1587-1634): "A Lullaby"

Giles Fletcher (1588-1623): "Who can forget—Never to be Forgot"

Friedrich von Spee, S.J. (1591-1635): "*Ecloga oder Hirten-Gespräch, darin
   zween Hirten, Damon und Halton, ihre Gaben erzählen, so sie dem
   Christkindelein schenken wöllen*"; also attributed to von Spee,
   "*Advent-Gesang*" and "*O Jesulein, o Gottes Sohn*"

Robert Herrick (1591-1674): "A Christmas Caroll, sung to the King in
   the Presence at White-Hall"; "An Ode on the Birth of our Savior"

Francis Quarles (1592-1644): "On the Infancy of our Savior"

St. Jean de Brébeuf, S.J. (1593-1649): "*Estennialon de tsonoue! Iesous ahatonnia*"—Carol of the Hurons

Christopher Harvey (1597-1663): "The Nativity"

Sister Violante do Ceo (1601-1693): "*Vilhancico*"

Paul Gerhardt (1607-1676): "*Zu Weihnachten*"

John Milton (1608-1674): *Paradise Lost,* XII, 360-371; *Paradise Regained,* I, 242-254

Richard Crashaw (1612-1649): "In the Glorious Epiphanie of Our Lord God"

Jeremy Taylor (1613-1667): "Hymn for Christmas Day, being a dialogue between three shepherds"; "A Hymn for Christmas Day"

Andreas Gryphius (1616-1664): "*Über die Geburt Christi*"

Henry Vaughan (1621-1695): "The Shepherds"

Thomas Traherne (1637-1674): "On Christmas Day"

Du Bois Hus (c. 1640): "*La Nuit des nuits et le Jour des jours*"

Edward Taylor (1642-1729): "Upon the Epiphany and the Three Wise Men"

Nahum Tate (1652-1715): "While shepherds watched their flocks by night"

Isaac Watts (1674-1748): "Miracles at the Birth of Christ"; "A Cradle Song"

John Byrom (1692-1763): "A Hymn for Christmas Day"

Charles Wesley (1707-1788): "The Incarnation"

Christopher Smart (1722-1771): "Epiphany"

Johann Wolfgang von Goethe (1749-1832): "*Epiphanias*"

Johann Peter Hebel (1760-1826): "*Die Mutter am Christabend*"

August Wilhelm Schlegel (1767-1845): "*Die heil'gen drei Könige*"

James Montgomery (1771-1854): "Nativity"

Clemens Brentano (1778-1842): "*Weihnachtslied*"

Alessandro Manzoni (1785-1873): "*Natale*"

Pope Pius IX (1792-1878): "*Tu scendi dalle stelle, o Re del Cielo*"

Annette von Droste-Hülsoff (1797-1848): "*Am Weihnachtstag*"

John Henry Cardinal Newman (1801-1890): "Epiphany-Eve"

Robert Stephen Hawker (1803-1875): "The Mystic Magi" and "Aishah Shechinah"

Pope Leo XIII (1810-1903): *In praeludio natalis Jesu Christi domini nostri*

Friedrich Hebbel (1813-1863): *Die Weihe der Nacht*

Frederick Faber (1814-1863): "Christmas Night"; "The Three Kings"

H. W. Longfellow (1817-1882): "The Three Kings"

Conrad Ferdinand Meyer (1825-1898): *Friede auf Erden*

Christina Rossetti (1830-1894): "Before the paling of the stars"; "A Hymn for Christmas Day"; *et alia*

Edwin Arnold (1832-1904): "At Bethlehem," from *The Light of the World*

William Morris (1834-1896): "Masters, in this hall"; "Outlanders, Whence come ye last?"

John Addington Symonds (1840-1893): "A Christmas Lullaby"

Alphonse Daudet (1840-1897): *La Vierge à la Crèche*

Robert Bridges (1844-1930): "Noel: Christmas Eve, 1913"

John Banister Tabb (1845-1909): "The Light of Bethlehem"

Alice Meynell (1847-1922): "Advent Meditation"

Eugene Field (1850-1895): "Hymn"; "Star of the East"; "Christmas Hymn"

Mary Coleridge (1861-1907): *Salus Mundi*

Louise Imogen Guiney (1861-1920): "A Carol"

W. B. Yeats (1865-1939): "The Magi"

Lionel Johnson (1867-1902): "Christmas"; "Carols"

Paul Claudel (1868-1955): *Chant de l'Épiphanie*

Hillaire Belloc (1870-1953): "Noel"; "Twelfth Night"

G. K. Chesterton (1874-1936): "The Nativity"; "The House of Christmas"; "The Wise Men"; "A Song of Gifts to God"

Rainer Maria Rilke (1875-1926): *Die Heiligen Drei Könige*; *Verkündigung über den Hirten*

Gertrud von le Fort (1876-1971): *Advent* and *Weihnacht* from *Hymnen an die Kirche*

Joseph Campbell (1879-1944): "The Magi"; "O Beauty of the World"; "I Follow a Star"; "By a Wondrous Mystery"

Konrad Weiss (1880-1940): *"Gott in der Krippe"*

William Carlos Williams (1883-1963): "The Gift"

Charles Williams (1886-1945): "Kings Came Riding"

Gabriela Mistral (1889-1957): *"Noel indio"*; *"Pinos de Navidad,"* and *"Estrella de Navidad"*

Werner Bergengruen (1892-1964): *"Die Hirten"*; *"Der mystische Tau"*

e.e. cummings (1894-1962): "from spiralling ecstatically this"

Leonard Feeney (1897-1978): "The Lonely Crib"; "The Holy One of Mary"

C. S. Lewis (1898-1963): "The Nativity"

Janet Lewis (b. 1899): "A Lullaby"

Langston Hughes (1902-1967): "Carol of the Brown King"

Countee Cullen (1903-1946): *"Christus Natus est"*

Louis McNeice (1907-1963): "Carol"

W. H. Auden (1907-1973):"For the Time Being: A Christmas Oratorio"

Kenneth Patchen (1911-1972): "I have lighted the candles, Mary"

Brother Antoninus (William Everson) (b. 1912): "Phoenix: Out of the Ash"; "Triptych for the Living"; "The Massacre of the Holy Infants"

John Frederick Nims (b. 1913): "Christmas"

Thomas Merton (1915-1968): "Carol"

Pierre Emmanuel (b. 1916): *Les Jours de la Nativité*

Charles Causley (b. 1917): "Innocent's Song"; "Hymn for the Birth of a Royal Prince"; "Sailor's Carol"; "The Sheep on Blackening Fields"; "The Animals' Carol"; "A Song of Truth"

# Appendix C

## Additional reading

Beach, Waldo. *Christmas Wonder: An Anthology of Verse and Song.* Philadelphia: The Fortress Press, 1973.

Federer, Konrad. *Weinacht der Welt.* Zürich: in Verlag der Arche [no date].

Freemantle, Anne. *Christmas Is Here. A Catholic Selection of Stories and Poems.* New York: Stephen Daye Press, 1955.

Grigson, Geoffrey. *The Three Kings.* Gordon Fraser, 1958.

Harrison, Michael, and Christopher Stuart-Clark. *The Oxford Book of Christmas Poems.* Oxford University Press, 1987.

Hayes, Albert M., and James Laughlin. *A Wreath of Christmas Poems.* New York: New Directions, 1972.

Keyte, Hugh, and Andrew Parrot. *The New Oxford Book of English Carols.* New York: Oxford University Press, 1992.

Lewis, D. B. Wyndam, and G. C. Haseltine. *A Christmas Book: An Anthology for Moderns.* New York: E. P. Dutton and Co., 1928.

Poston, Elizabeth. *The Penguin Book of Christmas Carols.* New York: Viking Penguin, 1986.

Rickert, Edith. *Ancient English Christmas Carols.* New York: Cooper Square Publishers Inc., 1966.

Shrady, M. L., *In the Spirit of Wonder.* New York: Pantheon Books, 1961.

Simcoe, Mary Ann. *A Christmas Sourcebook.* Chicago: Liturgy
   Training Publications, 1984.

Undset, Sigrid. *Christmas and Twelfth Night.* New York and Toronto:
   Longmans Green and Co., 1932.

*Westermann's Weinachtsbuch.* Braunschweig: Georg Westermann Verlag, 1949.

# Index

## By author and title

# Sophia Institute Press®

## Classics for a new generation of readers

Sophia Institute™ is a nonprofit institution that seeks to restore man's knowledge of eternal truth, including man's knowledge of his own nature, his relation to other persons, and his relation to God.

Sophia Institute Press® serves this end in a number of ways. It publishes translations of foreign works to make them accessible for the first time to English-speaking readers. It brings back into print many books that have long been out of print. And it publishes important new books that fulfill the ideals of Sophia Institute™. These books afford readers a rich source of the enduring wisdom of mankind.

Sophia Institute Press® makes high-quality books available to the general public by using advanced, cost-effective technology and by soliciting donations to subsidize general publishing costs. Your generosity can help us provide the public with editions of works containing the enduring wisdom of the ages. Please send your tax-deductible contribution to the address below. Your questions, comments, and suggestions are also welcome.

For your free catalog, call:

## Toll-free
## 1-800-888-9344

or write:
Sophia Institute Press®
Box 5284, Manchester, NH 03108
www.sophiainstitute.com

Sophia Institute™ is a tax-exempt institution as defined by the Internal Revenue Code, Section 501(c)(3). Tax I.D. 22-2548708.